WILLIAM H

A HUMAN DOCUMENT

Elibron Classics
www.elibron.com

Elibron Classics series.

© 2005 Adamant Media Corporation.

ISBN 1-4021-7317-2 (paperback)
ISBN 1-4021-3394-4 (hardcover)

This Elibron Classics Replica Edition is an unabridged facsimile of the edition published in 1892 by Cassell Publishing Company, New York.

Elibron and Elibron Classics are trademarks of
Adamant Media Corporation. All rights reserved.

This book is an accurate reproduction of the original. Any marks, names, colophons, imprints, logos or other symbols or identifiers that appear on or in this book, except for those of Adamant Media Corporation and BookSurge, LLC, are used only for historical reference and accuracy and are not meant to designate origin or imply any sponsorship by or license from any third party.

A HUMAN DOCUMENT

BY

W. H. MALLOCK

AUTHOR OF "IS LIFE WORTH LIVING," "A ROMANCE OF THE NINETEENTH CENTURY," ETC.

NEW YORK
CASSELL PUBLISHING COMPANY
104 & 106 FOURTH AVENUE

COPYRIGHT, 1892, BY
CASSELL PUBLISHING COMPANY.

All rights reserved.

THE MERSHON COMPANY PRESS,
RAHWAY, N. J.

INTRODUCTION.

THE following work, though it has the form of a novel, yet for certain singular reasons hardly deserves the name. It is based from end to end on authentic records of fact; and it is virtually a personal memoir of the most daring and unreserved kind—so unreserved, indeed, that I am justified in making the disclosure only because death, distance, and circumstance, as well as literary disguise, have placed the characters dealt with beyond all reach of recognition. That this is the case will be made quite plain to the reader by a short account of how I obtained my materials, what those materials were, and the manner in which they have been treated.

I happened to be staying at a country house on the Continent a year or so after the publication of a now celebrated book. That book was the "Journal of Marie Bashkirtseff"; and as several of the party then present were reading it, it was not unnatural that it should be continually discussed and alluded to. There was one lady, however—a Countess Z——, a Hungarian, whose interest in it struck me as being keener than on ordinary grounds could be accounted for; while sitting with her on a pleasant afternoon in a pavilion by the side of a lake, and talking idly of any triviality that suggested itself, she recurred to the subject so abruptly and with such an air of abstraction, that I felt convinced it was constantly occupying her mind. Her remark was not very striking, and it required no particular answer, so by way of showing her that I was civil enough to be attending, I gave expression to a thought which had often before occurred to me.

"What a pity," I said, "that a woman like Marie Bashkirtseff, with such resolute frankness, and such power of self-observation, should have died before her experiences were better worth observing. She often tells us herself that she has nothing in her life to hide A woman who can say that has not much to reveal. It does not mean merely that she has not lived badly—it means also that she has not lived at all."

My companion fixed her eyes on me with an odd look of inquiry.

"Do you remember this?" I went on. "There is one thing and one thing only which Marie Bashkirtseff seems to wince at recording; and that thing, she exclaims passionately, sullied her whole life. Do you remember what it was? It was a single kiss on the forehead which she gave to an uninteresting boy. A woman who can think herself sullied by a childish trifle like that knows no more of life than a man can know of partridge shooting who feels disgraced as a sportsman by a splash of mud on his shoe."

"Tell me," said the countess with a slight access of irony, "how deep in the mud must a woman walk before a man considers her progress interesting?"

"He doesn't want her," I said, "to walk in the mud at all. When you ask that question you are running away with a word. What he wants her to experience is not the dirt of life, but the depths. The woman we are speaking of had only paddled in the shallows, and she thought herself drowning when a ripple broke over her ankles. I confess I am irritated by this super-sensitive delicacy; and yet, after all, it is that very quality which, if she had ever really lived, would have made her Journal such a revelation. I wish," I went on, as my thoughts more or less ran away with me, "I wish that this woman, with all her moral daintiness, had been swept off her feet by some real and serious passion. I wish that with soul and body she had gone through the storm and fire; that what she had once despised and dreaded, had become the desire of her heart; and that she had found herself rejecting, like pieces of idle pedantry, the principles on which once she prided herself as being part of her nature. What an astonishment and what an instruction she would have been to herself during the process! Think how she would have felt each part of it—the degradation, the exaltation, the new weakness, the new strength, the bewilderment, the transfiguration! Could she only have known all this, and have written it down honestly, she then would have given us a human document indeed."

Countess Z—— remained silent for a moment or two. At last she said, "I am thinking over a practical matter. I possess a certain something, and I am thinking whether I will show it to you. Tell me," she went on with a laugh, "do you think you would care to see it?"

To this riddle only one answer was possible. "Anything which you think worth showing me I am sure I shall think worth seeing."

INTRODUCTION.

"Ah," she replied, "but you will have to do more than see it. This is something which you will have to pore and puzzle over, and if you don't take enough trouble about it to thoroughly try your temper, I shall discover how apathetic you have been, and consider you have abused my confidence. You are perhaps prepared to hear that what I speak about is a collection of manuscripts."

"Are they yours?" I asked.

"Only," she said, "in the sense that they are my property. They were left me by the writer, who died a few months ago. She was a beautiful woman, and you know something about her; but not much, or I can't tell what would have happened to you."

"Go on," I said; "this is indeed interesting."

"If you really meant," she replied, "what you were just now saying, it ought to be far more interesting to you; than you have the least reason to suppose. Shall I tell you what the manuscript is? It is an imaginary continuation of Marie Bashkirtseff's Journal, in which she is represented as undergoing the exact fate you were wishing for her. I suspect, too," she continued, "that it is something more than that. Indeed, I am certain that it is; but you must read it first, and I will talk it over with you afterward. If you care to have it, it shall be sent to your room to-night."

Countess Z—— was as good as her word. I was tempted for a moment to think she was even better, when, on going upstairs to bed, I saw lying on my table, not what I had pictured to myself—a small, unpretending packet, which I could have held in my hand, and put with my pocket-handkerchief under my pillow, but a

INTRODUCTION. vii

great folio volume bound like a photographic scrapbook, the sight of which filled me with dismay. When, however, I opened it, I was at once reassured and puzzled. It was a scrapbook in reality, not in appearance only; and its bulk was explained by the fact that its leaves were of thick cartridge paper, and that the manuscript, whose sheets varied in size and appearance, had been pasted on to these, with a liberal allowance of margin. I realized presently the reason of such an arrangement. The Imaginary Journal, as Countess Z—— had called it, was not entirely a journal, and was not entirely imaginary. I could see, it is true, that some single thread of narrative, in a feminine handwriting, ran through the whole volume; but this was broken by pages after pages of letters, by scraps of poetry, and various other documents, all in the handwriting of a man, and all—as it seemed—originals. "These," I said to myself, "are fragments of actual life"; and a glance which I took at a few scattered passages was enough to convince me that such was indeed the case. There was no mistaking the matter; for one or two of the letters bore traces of postmarks, which had indented them through their envelopes. The only thing that seemed strange to me was that any man in his senses should have cared to intrust to the post certain of the passages I had glanced at. My curiosity was so completely roused that I turned to the narrative, which I concluded would explain the whole. I began at the beginning; it was striking eleven when I did so; and I did not close the volume till nearly four in the morning, by which time I had read it through to the end.

It was a singular record, not only on account of its

contents, but of the manner in which it seemed to have been composed. The greater part of the narrative was just what I had been led to expect—an imaginary Journal of Marie Bashkirtseff, during an imaginary continuation of her life. This was written in French; and there was an obvious effort, at first, at reproducing the tone and manner of the original. It was an effort, however, which was not very successful; and the authoress soon abandoned it, or rather forgot to make it. As she did so, she became more and more interesting; until gradually, instead of reading the literary exercise of an amateur, I seemed to be listening to the voice of a living woman who was confessing to me. The very defects of her style, which, though generally clear and straightforward, yet often broke down with a sort of pathetic helplessness, contributed to this illusion. I felt each time this happened, that a woman's eyes were looking at me, and that her lips, as she spoke, had a deprecating smile on them, or that they trembled. Had she written far better the effect would have been far less vivid. To a critic, no doubt, her triumph would not have seemed a very legitimate one; but I found as I read on, that it became even more complete. The deeper the emotions she had to express, the more crude and fragmentary was the form in which she attempted to express them; and the result was that her baffled and crippled sentences, her abrupt transitions, and odd lapses of grammar, though they could hardly be said to constitute a good description of what she professed to have felt, seemed to be more than that; they seemed to be a visible witness of its reality, as if her language had been broken by it, like a forest broken by a storm, or as if it were some living tissue, wounded and quivering with sensation.

But there were further peculiarities about the narrative, besides those of style. Beginning as it did in the form of a journal, and maintaining for the most part this form throughout, it suddenly assumed at intervals that of an ordinary novel. The writer herself was spoken of in the third person; scenes were described at which she was not present; and the unspoken thoughts of a certain man were set forth by her as if he was avowedly a character of her own creation. When I first came upon a passage of this sort its effect naturally was to dispel the impression which had been growing on me, that the imaginary Journal was imaginary in name only. The whole thing at once seemed to be artificial, and instead of interesting fact, to be very childish fiction. Before long, however, I began to make discoveries, by which my original impression was not only restored, but strengthened. I have said that the woman's narrative was broken in many places by the insertion of various documents, evidently written by a man. The first of these was a letter which the imaginary Marie Bashkirtseff was made to say in her Journal she had received from a particular person. The sentiments expressed, and the events alluded to in it, all fitted completely the situation that had been described by her; but there was one discrepancy—every proper name was different. According to the Journal the letter came from St. Petersburg; in reality, it bore the address of a well-known club in Vienna. According to the Journal, the writer was a Russian; quite another story was betrayed by his clear signature; and all the subsequent documents by the same hand, whether they were letters, or verses, or, as some of them were, mere nondescript fragments, bore to the woman's narrative a relation substantially similar. This, however, is not the whole of the matter. One of the fragments I have mentioned seemed, as I read it, to be familiar to me; and I asked myself where I could have come across anything like it before. In a moment I recollected. It was in that very volume; it was in one of those parts of the narrative which were written in the form of a novel. The passage I am referring to described the thoughts of a man as he sat dejected and solitary, looking at a woman's photograph; and I had been surprised at the insight it displayed into the mysteries of the male heart. I now saw that the whole was taken almost literally from a confession that had been made by the very man himself who was in question. Nor did this case stand alone. I continually came afterward on others of the same kind. Descriptions, conversations, verses, philosophical and literary reflections, and pieces of self-analysis—things like these which occurred in the writings of the man, had, I discovered, been incorporated into the writings of the woman, she having changed hardly anything but the names. This change she had carried out consistently.

It may well be imagined that, after only one reading of it, a volume compiled so strangely left me in considerable perplexity; and for half the night I lay considering what was the explanation of it. But the following morning I went through it more carefully; and when, later in the day, I again met Countess Z——, I had come, as I was able to tell her, to a definite conclusion about part of it. So far as it related to the man, the story revealed in it was a true one; that man's life, for some reason or other, had had a special interest for the woman who wrote the Journal; by some means or other she had possessed herself of many of its secrets; and she had conceived the idea of at once describing and hiding it in what, with a reader, should pass for a work of fiction. Farther, she had wavered in her mind as to the form which this work should take—whether it should be that of a fictitious journal or of a novel; for it was evident now to me that the contents of the volume as they stood were merely a rough and experimental copy, interspersed with raw materials, of which as yet she had used part only.

"So much," I said to Countess Z——, "must be plain to anyone. That, however, is only one-half of the question, and as to the other half, I am altogether in doubt. The man's story is true, but then there is the story of the woman. Is that true also? Or was it merely constructed by the authoress in order to suit the dramatic requirements of the other? I have sometimes inclined to the first view, sometimes to the second. There are certain scenes and feelings described by her in a way in which a woman could not have described them—I constantly said this—if they had not been part of her own actual life; and yet, on the other hand, I constantly said also, would any woman, if they had been, have had the courage to describe them? There is another supposition which once or twice occurred to me, and that is, that though her whole story is true, it is the story not of the authoress but of some other woman, who had revealed it to her. I thought, you see, that though she might have shrunk from describing herself, she might yet have had nerve enough for a *post-mortem* examination of a sister."

"Your supposition is wrong," said Countess Z—— quietly. "It is her own story. She has changed, as you have observed, the names of places and people; and also a number of other accidental circumstances; but so far as essentials are concerned, she has, to the best of my belief, not written a word that is not absolutely true. In that volume you have her life, and the life of another, turned literally inside out."

"And do you mean to tell me," I exclaimed, "that a woman of position and reputation, a woman too so sensitive as she must have been, and in some ways so extraordinarily innocent, really proposed to publish such a confession about herself, with such a mere pretense of a veil thrown over her own identity? There are things in that Journal which the most callous woman would hide."

"There is nothing in that Journal," said Countess Z——, "which a callous woman could feel; and it is the sensitive women, and not the callous ones, for whom confession is sometimes a necessity. The veil, however, which you think so transparent, would really have been thick enough for every practical purpose. This hidden drama of which you have just seen the record, was unsuspected by anyone during the lifetime of the two chief actors. It is not likely to be suspected, now that they both are dead. The very people who knew them while it was in progress, and indeed took unconscious parts in it, would never, from any account of it, be likely to connect it with them, unless persons and localities were mentioned by their actual names; so the changes made by the authoress, slight as you may think them, would have been more than sufficient, supposing her book had been published, to have preserved her secret from even her own acquaintance. And now," Countess Z—— continued, "I will ask your opinon about this. I have several times wondered during the last few weeks whether someone might not be found who could take the volume in hand and do for my poor friend what she had herself intended to do with it—work up its contents into some presentable form, and publish it. Do you think that a book like that would be found generally interesting?"

"That would depend largely," I said, "on how it happened to be written. The whole of the materials would have to be recast; for as they stand they are not a story in any literary sense; though they enable us, or rather force us, to construct one out of them for ourselves. But supposing that the story in question were to be told in an adequate way—and by this I mean only one very simple thing; I mean in such a way as to impress the reader with the truth of it—no novel that I have read for years, would for me personally have half so much meaning or interest."

"I have thought," said Countess Z——, "of writing to our Hungarian novelist J——, and asking him to look at the manuscripts, and see if he could make anything out of them; but I have now got a new project, and you must tell me honestly what you think of it; for it is to make that proposal not to him, but to you. There are several reasons," she continued, "why, if you care to undertake it, you would be specially suited to the task. The characters, as you have seen, have a certain connection with England; and an Englishman would understand them far better than a Hungarian. There is one reason: here is another. You know Hungary, or at least certain parts of it; and it so happens that some of the places where you stayed are the very places in which some of the incidents of the story happened. But now I am coming to a better reason still. Do you remember that, when you were staying at Schloss S——, you made an expedition to Count D——'s villa, at N——, a house on the slope of a hill, just under a ruined castle?"

"How," I exclaimed, "could you possibly know that? For it was not—I am certain—one of the things I told you about."

"No," she said, "but Countess D—— is my sister. I often stay there; and a little white boudoir, into which I know you went, opening out of the hall, is my own room. You needn't stare at me as if you thought I was a witch. My sister and I arrived there the day after your visit. I heard of you from the housekeeper; and in particular I heard this. Of all the pictures—and there are many of them supposed to be interesting—you would look at none but three miniatures in my boudoir—three miniatures in a case, all of the same woman. You couldn't be got away from them."

"This is perfectly true," I said, "I see them distinctly still. The woman had a dress of a different color in each. There was a brown dress, a purple dress and a red one with white spots on it. And what did her face mean? Was it guilt, or innocence, or passion, or aspiration? It was a sort of chameleon, and it meant them all by turns. That, at least, is what I thought afterward. I only felt at the time as if there were some philter in the ivory."

"That," said Countess Z——, "is the woman who wrote the Journal. It is her life and soul that I am now preparing to commit to you. Ah," she exclaimed, "I have touched you, I see, at last! Do you consent? Will you refuse what I ask you? Come," she went on, "bring down the book into the library. We shall not be disturbed there, and we will look it over together."

I brought it. She turned to something which I had not before noticed—a pocket inside one of the covers, and she extracted from it a piece of thin note paper. "Look at this," she said. "You have probably not seen it. It is the dedication which the authoress meant to have prefixed to her book; and it will show you how completely you will be fulfilling her wishes if you will only write and publish that book as her proxy."

What she held out to me was merely a few lines. I recognized the hand with which the perusal had made me familiar; but, to my surprise, what I now saw was written not in French but in English, and not in the English of a foreigner. The Countess had called it a Dedication"; the writer herself had given it a different title, which was "Consecration." Then came some words, well known to an English reader, but seeming strange when appropriated here: "To the sole and only begetter of this volume." And then came what follows:

You by whose side I shall lie, in a wicker coffin like yours, with whose bones my bones shall mingle, and whose flesh I shall meet again in the sap of the violets above our grave, I have done my best, while waiting to come back to you in death, to perpetuate in this book neither your life nor mine, but that one single life into which both our lives were fused. Were my power as a writer equal to my love as a woman, that life should live in these pages, as it lived and breathed once in our now lonely bodies. I would make it live—all of it; I would keep back nothing; for perfect love casts out shame. But if anyone should think that I ought to blush for what I have written, I should be proud if, in witness of my love for you, every page of it were as crimson as a rose."

When I had finished reading this I found my companion looking at me with an expression of triumph at the interest which was no doubt visible in my face. "I told you," she said, "that you knew something of my authoress; and wasn't I right in adding that if you had known more, I should have been afraid to predict the consequences? Come," she went on, "have I not won my cause? You cannot refuse me now; your heart is in the work already."

"It is," I said. "I confess it. But still I foresee difficulties—some of them specially incident to writing such a book in English. Give me to-day to think the matter over; and to-morrow I will tell you what I can really do."

The difficulties which had first struck me, and which first engaged my attention, were those which, in spite of what Countess Z—— had said, I thought might be experienced in concealing the identity of the characters; and the following day I pointed many cases out to her, where more disguise would be necessary than a mere change of name. On second thoughts she was disposed to admit this; but, on the other hand, she now went on to explain to me a variety of things which the manuscript only imperfectly indicated, such as the position and circumstances of each of the characters mentioned in it, and the precise extent to which the salient facts of the story escaped the notice of the society in the midst of which they occurred. And the result was to convince me that she had been substantially right from the first, and that the book she was anxious I should attempt might, without any imprudence, be so written as to be minutely and literally true, not only in all essentials, but in point even of local color—indeed that many of the facts would be disguised most completely, if they were taken from the manuscript without any change at all.

That book accordingly is now offered to the reader. As to what the changes are which I have been obliged to make, I cannot say more, or the object of those changes would be defeated. For the method of narration and for the style, indeed, I am myself of course responsible; but whatever may be thought of this part of the book, and whatever else I may or may not have contributed to it, I can say of it at least one thing with confidence, even if it is not a piece of literature, it is a piece of life; it is genuinely a human document.

And this brings me to a very important point. It is precisely because the book is true in this wide sense that there are certain difficulties, as I said to Countess Z——, specially incident to its being produced in English. In the English fiction of to-day, it is a universal rule that the men, and especially the women, with whom the reader is invited to sympathize, shall always stop short in their relations to one another at a certain point, whatever may be their dispositions and circumstances. It is also a rule equally universal, that any grave transgression of the conventional moral code shall entail on its transgressors some appropriate punishment, or at all events that it shall not end in their happiness. In the present book neither of these rules is observed. The characters violate the first; their history violates the second; and the reason is that this book is true to life, while to a great part of life the rules are absolutely untrue. The fact remains, however, that in this country these rules supply to a numerous class of readers a sort of moral standard by which all fiction is judged; and the book is consequently one to which many people may raise objections. I think it best to admit this fact plainly; and to state, in a brief and general way, how I should answer such objections myself, supposing them to be really raised. I should not consider it a sufficient answer to say that every detail mentioned in it was taken from actual life; for it is quite possible so to select such details, as to misrepresent the life of which they formed a part, and to convey a false idea of human nature generally. This, in my judgment, is precisely what is done by M. Zola. His fault is not that he exhibits the operation of certain passions, which our English novelists forbear altogether to deal with. It is that he represents those passions as covering a larger field than they do; and that the other elements of life, which are of at least equal importance, are dwarfed by this treatment into a grotesquely false insignificance. This is not the fault, however, of such writers as M. Zola only. It is the fault of writers such as Miss Yonge also, and if we try both by the same severe standard, "The Daisy Chain" must be condemned for the same reason as "Nana."

Neither are true to life for each excludes one-half of it. No doubt "The Daisy Chain" has this point in its favor —that it is, as it was meant to be, a good book for children, whereas a book like "Nana" is a good book for nobody. But what is good for children is useless for men and women, who differ from children mainly in their inevitable experience of so much that we shelter childhood from even hearing of prematurely. To men and women, who are capable of observation and reflection and who are neither depraved nor abnormally innocent, life is essentially a combination of widely different elements. Whatever may be our definition of good or evil, and however remote as an abstraction the one may be from the other, we see that as realities they are everywhere in the closest contact, sometimes fretting each other, sometimes apparently united not only in the same society, but in the same people and in the same motives and actions; and the interest of life depends upon neither separately, but on the constant and ever changing relations between the two; the evil losing its meaning when considered apart from the good, and the good losing its meaning when considered apart from the evil. Hence it follows—and surely nobody can dispute the fact—that any picture of the one must be misleading and incomplete, unless it is part of a picture equally complete of the other. Now my case on behalf of the present book is this—that it presents us with a picture equally complete of both; and that its various details are not only true individually, but form collectively a true representation of life.

It may, however, still be urged by some that I have not so much as touched upon the important question yet. The important question, they may say, is not whether the book is true, but whether it is moral. My answer would be this—that if it is true in the sense I have just described, it is as moral or as immoral as life is, neither more nor less. If it is immoral to show, as actual life shows, that the hard and fast division between good and evil, which undoubtedly exists in the region of abstract theory, and which for certain purposes it is undoubtedly necessary that we should recognize, does not exist in the lives of average men and women; and farther, what is still more important, that good and evil fortune do not follow, in any invariable way, on what moralists classify as good and evil conduct, but are constantly apportioned, without any apparent reference to the conventional requirements of retributive moral justice; if it is immoral to show all this, then it must be admitted that this book is immoral. But in that case we must make another admission also—that life is immoral in precisely the same sense; that while moralists teach one thing, it teaches another, and that no picture of it is fit for good people to look at, in which half of its distinctive features have not been suppressed or altered.

If anyone takes this view of the case, I cannot, here at least, attempt to argue him out of it. I must content myself with saying that the view is not mine, but that I hold to the opposite and, indeed, the only other alternative. I believe that morality is only worth inculcating because, and in so far as, its motives, rules, and sanctions correspond to the realities of life considered in its entirety. I believe, therefore, that any picture of life, if only complete so far as its subject goes, will be sure to convey some moral or other, though what that moral is may vary with the minds that look for it. It will in any case be sounder than any that could be conveyed by illustrations manipulated for the special purpose of conveying it; and a complete autobiography of the conscience of a single profligate, were such a thing possible, would teach us more than a dozen descriptions of the selected pieties of saints. How far such teachings would, in their practical tendency, correspond with those which are conventionally called moral in this country is doubtful. Sometimes the correspondence between the two would be complete and striking; but sometimes the former would certainly contradict the latter, if not in their most important, at all events in their tenderest, points. This must be admitted as a general truth; but readers of the present book, which is all that we are here concerned with, if affronted by finding in it anything not moral in the conventional sense, will at all events be comforted by finding under the surface much that would coincide with the morals of the most conventional sermon. If they are scandalized by being shown that people who have many undoubted virtues can yet deliberately commit certain offenses, they may learn a sharp and salutary lesson in charity by being shown that people whom they would curtly classify as offenders may yet have virtues which perhaps in themselves are wanting. If they see consciences easy which they think ought to be troubled, they will see consciences troubled which superficially seem easy. They will see, in short, what ought to edify them more than anything, even if it does not happen to do so, that the sense of virtue and the practice of right conduct are far from being the monopoly of those who are technically virtuous. Finally, if the book is complained of because people who are not technically virtuous are shown in it to have been ultimately happy, as such people often are, I would point out that their happiness, such as it is, results from qualities in them which everyone must admire, and not from those of their actions, which perhaps most people will condemn.

A HUMAN DOCUMENT.

CHAPTER I.

In the early spring of the year 18— certain public events happened to have attracted to Vienna a considerable number of the English who had been spending the winter on the Continent; and the British Ambassadress was fully justified in saying, as she said one evening to a cluster of old friends, that though that year she would be unable to go to London, for the last fortnight London had come to her.

This remark was made in her own drawing-room, where the guests were slowly assembling for a dinner-party that was to be exclusively English.

"My dear," she went on regretfully, as she drew aside from the others a distinguished-looking woman, the complete whiteness of whose hair, due though it was to age, had the brilliant effect of powder, "I thought, of course, that you would have gone in with Julian; but the princess's coming has disturbed all my arrangements, and I'm afraid I shall have to consign you to old Lord R—— instead. I am more sorry than I can say; but you'll see that I've done my best for you. You will sit by his deaf ear, so you need not utter a word to him;

and on the other side of you you will have Robert Grenville."

"Mr. Grenville!" said the lady whose fate was thus announced to her, "I met him first when he was an attaché in Paris, when half the French ladies were in love with him, and he had just published some love-poems. Somehow or other one has not heard much of him lately. He ought, with his talents, to have made more noise in the world." Then, with her eyebrows slightly raised, and her lips for a moment smiling with a humorous self-contempt, "If that man," she said, "had been born a generation earlier, I fully believe I should have fallen in love with him myself."

"I've no doubt you would, my dear," said the Ambassadress with a certain trenchancy, not malicious itself but hinting a sense on her part of saying something that might be said maliciously.

"You will, therefore, be happy to hear that he is now in a fair way to make as much noise in the world as even his best friend could desire. Let us ask Julian." And she turned round to her husband. "Just look at him. He is quite absorbed in your niece. It is always with him a case of the 'eternal feminine.' Julian," she said, "Lady Ashford is asking about Mr. Grenville. She would like to hear how a poet is going to rise to fame."

The Ambassador was indeed engrossed in what seemed his most frequent occupation—that of talking to the youngest and prettiest woman in the room. When thus appealed to he made no answer for a moment, but murmured to his companion, in his low indolent voice, "Did you ever know a poet? If you didn't, you must keep your eyes open, and you will see one to-night eating his dinner opposite to you." Then, lifting himself from his seat and coming toward his wife, he put his hand on her arm with a charming air of devotion, and said to Lady Ashford; "So you are talking of Robert Grenville. Many people, most likely, will soon be doing the same. I had a letter yesterday from the Chancellor of the Exchequer, and he told me that never, in all his former experience, had he met anyone with such a natural genius for finance."

"Finance!" echoed Lady Ashford. "What on earth are you talking about? What has finance to do with Mr. Grenville the poet?"

"Our poet," said the Ambassador, "is unfortunately a poet no longer, and the crown that is now held out to him was never woven by the Muses. What has happened to him has been this: I thought that of course you had heard of it. Just before the opening of last autumn's session, the Chancellor of the Exchequer lost one of his secretaries; and found himself suddenly overwhelmed in a certain country house with more work than he could manage without assistance. Grenville, who was staying there also, offered to do what he could for him. He did so, and with results that astonished the Chancellor and himself equally. He continued to act as secretary for the whole of the next six months; and now, when Sir Jacob Jackson goes home in July, Robert Grenville will take his post at Constantinople. If he can deal with the difficulties which are accumulating and awaiting him there, he may easily find himself at once one of the foremost figures in Europe."

"Well," said Lady Ashford plaintively, "it's an odd metamorphosis. One could never have thought that—

what shall I call him? well, a drawing-room love-poet, was the sort of stuff out of which fate could make a financier."

"There are," said the Ambassador, "two sorts of love-poet—the one with whom poetry is a substitute for life; and the other with whom it is a mere expression of part of it. The one is a dreamer whose ambition is passionate writing; the other is a man of action whose ambition is passionate living; and if he writes about love it is simply for this reason, that love at the time is the principal part of life for him. That was Grenville's case; and you can see it in all his verses. You can see in every line what the man who wrote them was thinking about. He was not thinking about verses; he was thinking about a woman. That was their great charm. They were interesting because they showed the women who read them that the writer would have been an interesting lover. Now, dear Lady Ashford," he went on, "of course you are aware of this—that of all important businesses, love-making in the world is the one which requires most knowledge of the world; so I don't think we need wonder if a man who excelled in that should be able to turn his talent to other practical uses."

"Julian," said the Ambassadress, "when you have done your discourse on poetry, I want to inform you that here is Princess Plekonitz."

"My dear friend," exclaimed the Ambassador turning round, and looking as if he would take in his arms the figure that stood before him, "what ages since we met! The sight of you makes me young again."

The Princess was a short sharp-eyed woman of seventy, with a face which was bright with a kind of caustic benevolence, and on which age had rewritten the smiles of her prime in wrinkles. She was English, an heiress —the widow of a Hungarian magnate; and as soon as her host was tired of retaining both her hands, she began to look round the room as if searching for old acquaintances. She failed, however, to discover any, even with the aid of her gleaming eyeglasses, till the last guest having arrived, the movement was made for dinner. Then suddenly, as she was taking her host's arm, "Who's that?" she asked. "Isn't it Mr. Grenville— Robert Grenville—Bobby, I used to call him? Yes, it's you," she called out, as a man at a little distance, who was just claiming his companion, turned round with a smile. "It's me too. Go on; and come and talk to me afterward."

Robert Grenville experienced one immediate consequence of having attention thus pointedly drawn to him. Several rapid glances were cast in his direction, and he felt rather than saw that he was an object of general interest. However small may be a man's share of vanity, there is in this feeling something which is certainly not displeasing to him. Robert Grenville was less vain than most men; his vanity was not flattered, but he was conscious that his spirits rose a little, and he sat down to dinner with a sense that he had more to say than he had when a moment ago he was starting to leave the drawing-room.

This was fortunate for the lady of whom he had been given the charge. She was the daughter of the governor of ——, now on his way to England, and under some present shyness the airs and graces were visible which had claimed and repressed devotion in the halls of Government House. Grenville had a foreboding that conversation would not be possible with her, but he now felt nerved for all the demands of duty; and by the time she had freed her gloves from the embraces of a whole family of bangles, he had hit on a question which made his path clear for him. On the opposite side of the table was a man with a bulbous face, whom he remembered to have seen once perspiring with importance at the Foreign Office. He asked his neighbor—providentially in guarded language—if she knew who this gentleman was, hardly expecting that she could tell him; and she, with an arch smile and a little jerk of her head, said, "Don't you know? That's my *pater*—that's Sir Septimus Wilkinson." Then cheered by a sense of superior social knowledge, she continued, "Look there —that is Sir Theophilus Entwistle." And she pointed out, by a nod, a shining star of the Colonial Office, partially eclipsed for the time being by a napkin, the corner of which he was tucking inside his collar. Her eyes now made a careful tour of the table and with increasing buoyancy she presently proclaimed to Grenville that she could, as she expressed it, "tell him about nearly everybody." Hardly waiting for encouragement, she came out with the names of various distinguished and highly fashionable personages, assigning a face to each name as she did so. The names were correct, and the people named were present, but she was not successful in putting the two together; and Grenville was for a moment struck dumb with astonishment when a certain old dowager, the fattest woman in London, was pointed out to him as her daughter, the flower of last year's season. He was, however, far too good-natured a man to confuse his informant by any blunt and cruel correction; but, adroitly pretending not to have understood her meaning, he managed to set her right without showing that he had discovered her to be wrong. All this made a good deal of conversation; but at last the subject was exhausted, and Grenville's wit was failing him, when a spotty little attaché, Miss Wilkinson's other neighbor, caught her bead-like eye and soon relieved him of her attention.

"Mr. Grenville, I am at last able to speak to you." The words were Lady Ashford's and they sounded like a musical bell. Grenville turned round; his entire bearing changed, and his face took the look of interest which he had been just trying to simulate. "That young person," Lady Ashford continued, "seems to me to have made you very vivacious. She was your lawful partner, but I'm sure you have done your duty by her, so you must now devote yourself to me and help to deliver me from mine."

"Ah," replied Grenville, "this is really delightful. I always thought talking to you a pleasure that could never be improved upon; but to-night, it will have the added charm of an infidelity."

Lady Ashford's age was not far from seventy, but much of the beauty for which she once was famous remained with her, and there still floated in her eyes a St. Martin's summer of youth.

"Is this," she said, looking at Grenville, "the result of a poet's philosophy? But you're no longer a poet—I ought to have remembered that; and now I remember that I want you to tell me what you are. Come, I must have your whole story out of you—the metamorphosis of the poet into the man of action. When did the change begin? How did you grow practical?"

Grenville was a man who hated to talk about himself; but Lady Ashford was at once so firm and so fascinating that she had soon extracted from him the information she asked for.

"Well," she said, when he had finished, "and so it all came to this. The world, when first you entered it, was enchanted for you by two necromancers, love and religion, who colored it with colors and filled it with objects of ambition, which gradually, as years went on, dissolved or faded from your sight, till at last you woke up to what you now consider realities. The first reality that came home to you was the want of some more money; accordingly you began to dabble in what you describe as business; and you found that your wits were far sharper than you expected. You hadn't however made a fortune in the first six weeks, and you were consequently beginning to think that real life was a failure, when you suddenly stumbled into a by-road to success—a sort of success that is brilliant beyond your hopes, and that gives you a promise of fortune and fame as well. Now to a man ambitious like you—for you always were ambitious—Mr. Grenville, you need not deny it; I have not studied men's temperaments for nothing—to a man ambitious like you, this luck ought to be intoxicating. Still it is not exactly success as you used to dream of it. You dreamed of it with the feelings of a poet; you achieve it as a practical man. I want you to tell me if it disappoints or satisfies you."

"When it comes," said Grenville, "I will tell you with great pleasure; but I am not aware that I have yet succeeded in anything."

"You have the opportunity of succeeding," said Lady

Ashford, "and other people know you have; you excite expectations, though you have not yet satisfied them; and that, to a man in your position, is success in its most flattering stage. You always were a figure of some interest in society; all of a sudden you are beginning to make a stir in it. I had realized this to-night before you entered the drawing-room. I saw it afterward in the way in which people looked at you. I heard it in their voices when they pronounced your name. You cannot pretend you were unconscious of the same thing yourself. I was told long ago, by somebody who ought to have known, that nothing is so sweet to a man as this first breath of applause, that it makes him feel as if his life were beginning to rise on wings. The dawn of fame must be like the dawn of love. I used often to say that to myself. I want you to be honest with me, and tell me your own experience."

"Well," said Grenville with a laugh of real embarrassment, "if you really wish for honesty, I will expose myself by admitting that—I hardly know how to put it— that I have a sort of sense of success in me, more or less like what you mention; and, I suppose it pleases me. Yes—yes, of course it does. I have so long thought and felt to so little purpose, that there is something exhilarating in the knowledge that at last I am about to act; and in the hope that I shall not, as I began to think I should, pass through the world leaving no mark behind me, having done nothing, and having been nothing. I admit too," he went on in a lighter tone, "that I am becoming conscious of a certain fuss being made about me. What trifles in themselves these little things are! And yet I am bound to confess that they have the same effect on me that a glass of champagne has on a man who has been long tired. I admit so much; but I admit nothing more. As to feeling as if I were going to rise on wings—I might have felt that once, but I certainly do not now. My wings by this time have hardly a feather left on them, though originally they were plumed with illusions bright as a bird of paradise. And as to the dawn of fame being like the dawn of love——"

"Well?" said Lady Ashford.

"As to that," he replied, "I can say nothing. What is love like? I cannot even remember. You look as if you didn't believe me; but I am not talking for effect. I have known the experience—the beginning, the middle, and the end of it, till I am as familiar with it, in one way, as I am with the journey to Brighton; but the impulse that made me undertake the journey is gone. I cannot even recall it."

Lady Ashford looked at him for a few moments in silence and then said, "Never mind; one day it will return to you. The real story of your life, Mr. Grenville, is still to come."

"I don't think so," said Grenville laughing. "All the same you are like an angel when you make the prophecy; and I—well, I hear it like Sarah behind the tent-door. No, no; the impulse is gone forever; and the only thing now that even faintly suggests it to me, is the longing produced in the mind by certain aspects of nature—the miraculous blue, for instance, of certain mountains or of the sea, a blue alive, like the blue in the veins of a woman's hand, allures me—maddens me— I don't know what it does to me. It makes me wish to be melted into it, and lost in it."

"If you can still feel all that," said Lady Ashford, "about salt water and hills, your days of feeling are not numbered yet. You think they are, because you have felt often; and you probably flatter yourself that these past attacks of the fever are a sort of inoculation which will keep you safe for the future. That may be the case with some men, but I am sure it is not so with you."

"And why," asked Grenville, with a certain natural curiosity, "why do you think it is not so with me?"

"Because," she said, "in spite of your good spirits in spite of your sense of success, I see a want in your eyes, I hear a want in your voice, which a woman recognizes, and of which she knows the meaning. The reason why love, thus far, has made so little impression on your memory, is not that you found so little in it, but that you looked for so much more; and this *much more* your nature is still waiting for. Listen, and let me teach you a small fragment of philosophy. Some of the women— I hope you will not be shocked at me—some of the women who have loved best have been women who found that they could not love their husbands. And why? They have learnt how much they longed to give and receive, by realizing how much one man could neither understand or give. People talk about first love; but what they talk about is a fiction just as the Golden Age is. First love is really like a first attempt on the fiddle. The magic and the music only come with experience. To love successfully you must often have loved in vain. You think this is a paradox, but it isn't. To make love complete—you may take a woman's word for it—it must be not only a giver of joy, but a healer of sorrow also; a resurrection of hope rather than its birth.

A boy's love may be life; a man's love is another life. This, Mr. Grenville, is the love which you are waiting for; or, if you like it better, which is somewhere waiting for you. And you may trust me in this, that when such love comes to a man, the passions of youth can show nothing to equal it. Don't despise my prophecy, because it comes from an old woman. You will find your fate; and old as I am I still remember mine."

"Yes," said Grenville, half involuntarily; "but you are a woman, and a woman who has once loved and remembers it can never be old."

"And a man," said Lady Ashford, "is always young, so long as a woman who is young loves him."

"Unfortunately," said Grenville laughing, "no young woman loves *me*." But then he suddenly checked himself, and went on in a different tone: "Your prophecy, Lady Ashford, is charming. It has only one fault, and that is, I cannot believe in it. Do you remember how just now you summed up the biography of my youth? You said that love and religion were two necromancers who had enchanted life for me. You were wrong. The real necromancer was the Imagination, which we used to think was the child of the other two, but which science and experience at last show us to be their parent. The children die of shame when we discover their parentage; and the Imagination itself cannot survive its children."

The conversation was here arrested by a sharp and startling sound. The chimney of a large lamp, which was in front of Grenville, had broken; some disturbance was caused by the servants' removing it from the table; and when Grenville again was in a position to speak or listen, Lady Ashford's ear had been captured by her other neighbor.

"And so that is Mr. Grenville, to whom you have just been talking?" Lord R—— was saying slowly, in the loud penetrating tone which deaf people, who require it to be applied to themselves, are not unfrequently accustomed to apply to others. Like many deaf and elderly people also, Lord R—— seemed always to be living in a little world of his own; and he had a charming habit of discussing people who were close to him, as if he were as much out of their hearing as they were out of his. "A very clever, promising young man," he went on. "I knew his father intimately—a very, very, very clever young man."

Grenville judiciously tried to escape from his own praises, and fixed his attention on the opposite side of the table. He found no difficulty in keeping it there. For the first time he saw an object facing him, which up to now the lamp had entirely hidden. It was the young girl—Lady Ashford's beautiful niece—to whom, before dinner, the Ambassador had been so gallantly devoting himself. It was impossible not to be struck by her—by her dazzling skin, by her dark melancholy eyes, and still more by an indefinable something—a something in her expression, her dress, her bearing—which gave her, despite her girlhood, the air of a married woman. Sitting next to her was Sir Septimus Wilkinson, talking to her with a voluble but elephantine eagerness, and giving point to his eloquence by gesticulating with his thick fingers. She, at the moment when Grenville first caught sight of her, was looking down with a sort of contemptuous self-possession, and amusing herself with examining her own beautiful hands. A moment later, and for a moment only, he saw her glance up at the shapeless face close to her, as if doubting and wondering whether a thing like that could be really made of the same flesh and blood as herself. Rapid as the glance was, Grenville felt that he understood it. The second after the girl's eyes met his own. As they did so, they seemed to expand softly, a certain light flashed up out of their depths, and there was the slightest undulation imaginable in the lines of her scarlet lips. Then all was over; she coolly turned away from him, and with a condescending animation began to address Sir Septimus.

No sooner had this happened than he was once more conscious of his own name being mentioned in tones as audible as before. "And now," Lord R—— was saying, "he's going to be married—that is to say, if he succeeds in his new career." Lady Ashford tapped him on his threadbare sleeve with her fan, doing her best to stop him. He took it for encouragement, and his voice became even louder. "The young lady's Lord Solway's niece—Lady Evelyn Standish—and if she marries with her uncle's consent she will have a considerable fortune. He will consent if Mr. Grenville succeeds; he told me so himself, but the matter is not yet to be spoken about."

Lady Ashford did the only thing to be done. She stopped any further disclosures by turning abruptly from the speaker; and she fixed her eyes with an odd look upon Grenville. There was embarrassment in them, and amusement in them, and also a wondering and half-reproachful inquiry.

"Mr. Grenville," she said, "this revelation is a judgment on you. Here is the man who never can love again. When we were talking just now, you were arguing under false colors."

"No," said Grenville gently, "I think not. If I marry I could still give my wife affection, but not—— Never mind! Let us talk no more about it."

"I'll tell you," said Lady Ashford, "what I should advise your doing. If you don't keep a diary, begin one this very night. Put down in it all that you feel now, being quite honest, and, if you can be—which I don't think you could be—quite clear. The time will come when you will laugh as you look back at it. Or perhaps you won't laugh. Perhaps you will do something else."

"Do you think," said Grenville, "that I shall only learn to love, by finding out that I cannot love my wife —whom, I may as well tell you, I have not yet asked to marry me? But come—let us drop *me*. As a subject, I must be quite exhausted. Suppose we talk about that lovely young lady opposite. I never saw such a pair of eyes in my life. Who is she?"

"She is my niece—Juanita Markham. Her mother was a Viennese. She has come here to see her relations. Yes—she has beautiful eyes—poor girl! She, too, Mr. Grenville, has all her life before her."

"And what," said Grenville, "is the fate you predict for her? Do you think that she, before she learns to love, must find out that she cannot love her husband?"

"I hope not," said Lady Ashford with sudden sadness. "There are many things which we excuse in ourselves, and which we should yet dread for our children. See—we are moving. We all go out together. There is Princess Plekonitz looking at you over her shoulder."

Grenville rose from his seat with a mind curiously

exhilarated. The drawing-room, when he reached it, had a brilliance for him which he had not noticed in it before; and roused some forgotten sense in him of the pride and the possibilities of life. He was soon surrounded by certain of the more distinguished guests; and though he knew them all well, and had long been accustomed to their civilities, they seemed, when they now addressed him, to be offering him an unfamiliar tribute. The apple of ambition was an apple which, in early youth, he had constantly looked up to, expecting that it would fall into his lap; it did not do so, and he had been slowly ceasing to think about it; but now, all of a sudden, it was close to him—it was actually at his lips, and his palate woke from its torpor, as the scent entered his nostrils.

From one flattering moment he passed on to another. What noiseless trifle can be more flattering to a man, than to find that the eyes of a woman, for whose attention others are contending, have been fixed on and following him, in the hope that he would attend to her? Grenville found this presently, in the case of Princess Plekonitz. There was a circle round her of people talking, or waiting to talk to her; but as soon as his eyes met hers, he saw it was himself she was thinking about. She beckoned him to her sofa with a movement of her fan and of her eyebrows; and the others, as he came up to her, separated. A couple of young men, however, did not go far, and he soon understood the reason; for sitting beside her on the sofa was the beautiful Miss Juanita Markham.

The Princess with effusion held out a wrinkled hand to him. She expressed a vivacious pleasure at thus unexpectedly seeing him; she recalled the old times when he had stayed at her house in England; and complimented him on his prospects in a way that would have sounded fulsome if the strong foreign accent, which she had acquired in living abroad, had not sufficed to confer a peculiar privilege on her English. All the time, however, that this was going on, though he listened and responded with really genuine feeling, he could not prevent a certain part of his consciousness being occupied with Miss Markham, and the fate of her two admirers. These last he had taken in at a glance. They were indeed attached to the Embassy, and he more or less knew both of them. They were well-bred young men, with the quietest manners imaginable; and if ordinary expensive dissipation means knowledge of life, they were probably right in flattering themselves that they were complete men of the world; but the girl's manner to them—a manner even quieter than their own—reduced each of them—Grenville could plainly see this—one after the other, in his own estimation, to a boy. Their first observations had been made with a smiling confidence. She had smiled also, and replied with complete civility; but joined to that civility was a yet more complete indifference, which seemed to produce, as it were, some chemical change in their characters. They blushed; they repeated their words; their laughs became doubtful and apologetic; and they presently found that nothing was left for them but to retreat with an air that betrayed discomfiture, while it aimed heroically at indifference.

"Listen," the Princess was by this time saying to Grenville; "the thing is quite simple: I will tell you all the particulars."

Whatever the particulars were they threatened to be long in telling; and Grenville, who had been standing hitherto, unconsciously scanned the sofa, as if to see whether there was room for him to be seated. Miss Markham, with extraordinary quickness, caught the meaning of his look and, raising her eyes to his with a full unflinching softness, moved so as to make a place for him between the Princess and herself.

"Thank you," he said, as he sat down; "I hope I am not crushing your dress."

"You are not," she replied, with a smile on her lips which were half parted. "But I think you have done one thing. Do you see what it is? You have hurt a feather of my fan." And, as if to explain the injury thus complained of, with a movement that might have seemed accidental, she drew the feather across his hand.

"Allow me to look at it," he said, with a slight accent of ceremony. "I trust I have done no harm." And he offered, as he spoke, to take the fan from her to examine it. But she, giving the feather a little semi-petulant pull, said, "No, after all I think it has not been broken. And showing him for a moment the faint remains of a smile, she folded her fan before her and gave her attention to the carpet.

This little episode over, and it did not occupy a minute, Grenville turned to the Princess, and seemed at once to forget it, in the interest of the subject which he was soon busy discussing with her. It was a subject, as anyone might have seen, who caught any fragment of the conversation, involving the settlement of many practical details; and anyone might have seen also that a conclusion was at last arrived at about it, which was highly satisfactory to both the parties interested, and gave to Grenville, indeed, a look of greater excitement than his face had shown before during any part of the evening.

At this juncture there was a movement of some of the guests departing. Lady Ashford was one of them. Coming toward the sofa, in order to call her niece to her, she began speaking to Grenville, who arose to say good-by. And now the entertainment yielded him its last incident. The niece, like the aunt, had turned toward him also, as if to include herself in a common process of leave-taking; and then, with a look in her eyes of deliberate hesitation, she held out her hand to him, and took his in a lingering clasp.

As soon as she was gone, he turned round to the Princess. "You told me," he said, "that I had new prospects before me. The prospect which you hold out to me is the newest and most fascinating of all."

CHAPTER II.

GRENVILLE, that night in his bed, found himself pleasurably restless, as he had hardly found himself since his earlier London seasons, when he walked home from balls through the dewy stillness of Piccadilly, with music and palm trees in his memory, some girl's voice in his heart, and the cool, dim primrose of the summer morning in his eyes. He made many efforts to sleep, but just as each seemed succeeding, some fresh thought would touch him, which provokingly flattered him into wakefulness; so that at last he got up again, and, partially redressing himself, he prepared to act on the only one of these thoughts which was at the present moment capable of being put into action. "I will do," he said to himself, "what Lady Ashford told me to do. I will begin a diary. I will describe myself to myself. I will make a chart, as it were, of my own present situation. Some day or other the reading of it may keep me awake. At any rate, the writing of it will now help me to sleep."

He found a note-book in his dressing bag sufficiently suitable for his purpose; the earlier pages, indeed, being full of memoranda, but the greater part being blank.

"The day after to-morrow," he began abruptly, "I am going to do something entirely strange to me and unexpected, which makes me feel like Tannhäuser with the Horsel suddenly opening to him. But this I must come to presently. I must start with what is more important.

"For the last eight or nine months, a crisis in my life has been preparing itself. To-night, for the first time, I feel fully conscious of it. Let me consider.

"I was always ambitious. Lady Ashford was right there; but, in saying this, let me do myself one piece of justice; for I *will* be just to myself. Ambition with me was only part of a wider hunger or aspiration, just as passion with a true lover is only a part of love. Passion alone is a cloud that hides the sky. Passion, when a part of affection, is a cloud crimson with sunrise. By the way, how easily that slipped from my pen; and yet, though I know it is true, it hardly is a truth that I feel. It is the sort of thing I should have written in the days when I experienced love. I suppose it comes into my mind now, because I am now undergoing an excitement somewhat similar, though the cause is so very different. Again—what have I written? Why, the very thing that Lady Ashford said to me at dinner. 'The dawn of fame,' she said, 'must be like the dawn of love'; and I laughed at her. Could she only see this diary, the turn to laugh would be hers. However, to go back to my ambition, what I mean to say for myself is this: that, though I longed to receive the external insignia of success—fame, consideration, place, and personal deference, I longed to deserve these quite as much as to receive them. Had I deserved them without receiving them, I should perhaps have despised life. Had I received them without deserving them, I should certainly have despised myself.

"Well—let me go on, continuing to be quite honest.

Always, so long as I can remember anything, I have had in my blood—I can describe it in no other way, a consciousness that I was a person who for some reason ought to be a personage. To me this seemed to be simply in the fitness of things. It is a fitness however that I have been always missing. Well-born and well-connected as I am, I have been without the means of distinguishing myself; and not to be distinguished, for a man like me, is a humiliation. It is to have fallen from an estate to which my hopes instinctively had raised me. In one's prime such a condition may be bearable, when social life still possesses its piquancy; but in maturer age—above all in old age, what a wretched thing would be such a life, and such a position as mine. My early fame as a poet is already nearly evaporated, like stale scent on a pocket-handkerchief. I represent a family that at last is as good as ruined. My mortgaged property yields me fourteen hundred a year, half of which I give to two helpless relations. My house is let to a brewer; and I live in a London lodging. How often have I shuddered at certain old men of fashion, with no home except a London lodging and their clubs, and with no life except dining, shooting, and visiting with a dwindling circle of friends; and I have seen in their old age a flattered foreshadowing of my own.

"But now, all has changed. I feel as if a fog had lifted; or as if, after long walking on sand, I had suddenly gained firm ground. I am in a fair way now to making myself really distinguishable; for a time at all events I shall receive a considerable income; and whatever advantages I thus gain, I may hope to consolidate them by a marriage which will not only bring me fortune, but a home and affection also. Let me jot down the facts on which this hope is founded. Lady Evelyn Standish I knew well when she was a child. A year ago, I met her again, a grown-up young lady. I met her often; but I did not give much thought to her, till I gradually became conscious that whenever I spoke in her presence, she listened to me; and that she constantly followed me with her frank guileless eyes. Hers is the kind of charm that one only sees if one looks for it; but the moment I saw it, it was a charm that drew me toward her, because—and in this I do not think I deceive myself—for some reason or other she was herself drawn toward me. The idea of a marriage with her soon shaped itself in my mind; but it was an idea which at that time I put aside as impossible. I knew that if she married with the approbation of an uncle, who is her guardian, she would in all probability have a considerable fortune, but neither to her nor to him would I present myself as a penniless fortune-hunter. Then my chance came; then my prospects changed; and without delay, though not without diffidence, I approached her guardian, and explained myself completely to him. He received me with a kindness that was beyond all my expectations; and if I do not, within the next six months, disappoint both myself and him he will fully sanction me in doing my best to win her. And he will do more. He will do what is a complete surprise to me. He will—that is, supposing the marriage happens—settle the property on her which marches with my own; and he will make arrangements by which, within a measurable time, my own may be freed from the greater part of its encumbrances. Can this be true? It all seems to me like a dream; and yet it seems to me at the same time less as if I were dreaming, than as if I were waking up to reality.

"I feel as if my personality were at last acquiring a body; or as if my limbs had long been bound, and were at last free and I could use them, moving weights with my arms, and realizing the power of my muscles.

"And now I come to the point for the sake of discussing which I was recommended to begin this diary. I am brought to it naturally. I have spoken about a wife. What are my feelings about love? At this moment they are so slight and so lukewarm, that I am actually irritated by the mere idea of discussing them. This sounds a strange confession to make, after just confessing myself intent on a happy marriage; but it is not so strange as it sounds. Let me be bold and explain myself by a paradox. I believe I am fit to marry, for this precise reason that I can no longer love. For by love, as I use the word now, and as Lady Ashford used it, what do we mean? We mean that despotic emotion which claims to extinguish, and which does extinguish while it lasts, all other emotions as the sun extinguishes a candle; which claims not to complete and crown the other blessings of life, but to supersede them. That is the love of which I have ceased to be capable; and I say well that I am now fit to marry, because I am no longer capable of it. For let me look the matter in the face fairly. The life of a man like myself ought to be largely in his work; unless it is so, it will be incomplete. But if you love a woman in the way I speak of, every interest is a rival to her; every interest is a wrong. Such love creates sins, just as the Scotch Sunday does. It turns a career into a kind of mental adultery. For a man like myself, then, the love that would absorb all life, is not fit to occupy any part of it. To love intensely is to be always saying one's prayers: and a man like myself must labor as well as pray. I am thus fortunate in being able to say this of myself—that I can hardly now conceive of love as a thing that should practically alter the general arrangements of my life, though I cannot only conceive but long for an affection that shall complete them. Yes—now I come to another part of these confessions; and I confess I make it with greater comfort to myself. Yes—I have done with love; but there is another feeling—we may call it not love but affection—which condescends to accommodate itself to circumstances, and to take its luck along with them. It does not complain, like an unreasonable woman in a railway-carriage, if, when the train is full, it cannot have a compartment to itself: nor does it ask that others should be crushed together, in order to leave it the luxury of two seats; but taking quietly such place as may be vacant for it, it insensibly humanizes and blesses its fellow-travelers instead of trying to push them out of the windows. Such an affection I can not only understand, but I long to give and receive it. That I have it to give, I know. That I shall receive it, I hope. It will not transfigure life with 'the light that never was on sea or land'; but it will be the light and warmth of a hearth that makes the chamber of life habitable, and which robs even the shadows of their mysteries, their coldness, and their gloom."

In writing these last words Grenville had turned over a page; and was about to proceed, when something suddenly checked him. "What on earth," he exclaimed "is here?" The cause of his exclamation was some lines scribbled in pencil. They were faint and not very legible, and he moved the book toward the candle. It was only when he had done this, that he saw them to be in his own handwriting, and also recognized them as verses. With puzzled curiosity he began deciphering them. "Can these be mine?" he said to himself. "Yes—they certainly must be. And yet when did I write them? To whom did I write them? When was I in a mood of mind about anyone like what they try to express? Stay—I think I have it. 'Salt seas'—'cinerarias!' Yes—I remember now, but it merely comes back to me like a dream. As the verses are here," he continued, "I may as well write them in. They will be a witness in my diary, either for or against, the kind of character which I have now outgrown."

The verses in question were as follows:

> Faith may live, though long doubts chill it ;
>   Charity will suffer much ;
> But for Hope—a touch can kill it,
>   And it rises at a touch.
>
> Where the cinerarias glisten
>   In your garden by the sea,
> At my side you once would listen,
>   Till your cheek was close to me.
>
> Where your caverns breathe and murmur
>   With the salt sea's sound and scent,
> Day by day your hand was firmer
>   On my arm : until I went
>
> Whispering in imagination
>   To your image in the air,
> All that love can teach to passion,
>   All that both can learn from prayer.

> Is there nothing—nay, come near me !
>   Look me in the face to-day !—
> Nothing which, before you hear me,
>   Tells you all I die to say?
>
> Where your cinerarias glisten,
>   Come, and I will tell you. Come!
> Lean your ear once more and listen.
>   What is this? My lips are dumb.
>
> Do your eyes, whose kind attention
>   Holds me, as when last we met,
> Not remember——? But why mention
>   What I see your eyes forget?
>
> Let it go ; for now I know
>   All those seeds of vain desire
> In your memory melt like snow ;
>   But on mine they lie like fire !

Grenville read the verses over several times, smiling incredulously. He then took up his pen again. "What wretched words for songs," he wrote, "can be buoyed up into poetry, like a ship lifted by a tide, if they are set to passionate music, and sung with feeling. And that which music does for a song written by somebody else, may, in the case of the writer himself, be done for it by his own emotions. These verses of mine, for instance—I have no doubt, when I wrote them, there was some emotion at work in me, which made them for me full of sound and meaning. But now the emotion is gone, and they seem to me like something withered. They have lost a body, or they have lost a soul. They are like the ghost of a poem, or the fossil of a poem. They are in fact a type of my former self; and an illustration of how it survives in me—that self I have outgrown so utterly.

"And yet not so. I traduce myself. I can no longer love, it is true; but the fact that I have loved, survives in its present effect on me, making me a different man to what I should have been otherwise. I am not indeed haunted by any personal regrets. I am completely cured of every individual passion. The state of the case is this. All the women I have known, seem in my memory to have become one, who has all depths and varieties of temperament, of insight, and of feeling, united in her: and this woman—or rather this womanhood—though silently withdrawing itself below the horizon of youth, is not lost: it colors the air of maturity with all the colors of a sunset. When the color goes, will age show the light of heaven?"

At this point Grenville paused. Then he began several sentences, scratching each out when he had written it, and again pausing. Then he proceeded thus:

"Most men love, I suppose, but the love-memories of most of them are like decayed, or at best like dried, rose leaves. The love memories of others are like attar of roses. For these men, love in this changed form penetrates all their lives, breathing among their thoughts like the breath of spring in a wood, sometimes like the breath of autumn, giving a soul to everything. This is the secret of my own feeling for nature. That feeling does not, as Lady Ashford said it did, mean that I shall love again. It means only that I have loved already; and each beautiful prospect—a purple Italian twilight, or old silvery town shining in mist on a mountain-side— is a keepsake of some lost passion, and inspires life, as passion did, with what really is the essence of youth—a sense of possibilities still waiting for fulfillment.

"I see that, without thinking about it, I have mentioned two things together—an Italian twilight and an old town. There was more in that than mere accident, for the two things represented by them are curiously and closely connected—Nature and the historic past. Just as Nature suggests the lost romance of ones' own life, so does the past represent romance in general. Each charms us by producing an illusion which will never be destroyed, because each presents us with a dream which will never again be a reality. We see the present reflected in the past shining like a Golden Age, as we see the sky in water.

"This is no mere imagined pleasure, though it is due to the imagination. It is real, it is delightful, it is invigorating. My good spirits at this moment are mainly due to the fact that unexpectedly I am going to have a fresh taste of it. Here comes my story. I have worked so hard during the past eight or nine months, that I found myself growing gradually quite unable to sleep—not, however, for the reasons that are keeping me awake now. What keeps me awake now is my imagination holding a holiday; what has been keeping me awake lately has been the refusal of my brain to take one. Schedules, statistics, calculations, drafts of financial schemes—these are the things that have haunted me at night like furies, driving sleep from my heavy eyelids as vigilantly as they could, and turning such short dreams as they could not keep away into weary visions of pages of official paper, or grotesque echoes of official conversations. My health then came to be such that I was ordered a six weeks' rest, the first few days of which were to be merely a change of work, consisting of some easy official business at Vienna. The remainder of the time was to be altogether my own. The Princess to-night asked me how I meant to spend it. 'At first,' I said, 'I was divided between two plans. One was an expedition along the Dalmatian coast, the other was a desultory wandering along certain less-known parts of Northern Italy, I am devoted,' I said, 'to old things—to old towns, old castles, old palaces, to the spectacle of old peasant life where it still remains unchanged, and old national costumes still flashing in embrowned market-places, and in Dalmatia or Italy I meant to have seen my fill of them. Here, however, at Vienna, I happened to learn from some friends of certain wonderful castles in Bohemia, and among the Karpathian Mountains.'

"The Princess screwed up her eyes with a smile of benign contempt.

"'Bohemia,' she said, 'and the Karpathian Mountains! Stuff! If you want to see castles, come and stay with me in mine, in Hungary, and I will help you to see as many others as you wish. Don't laugh like that. When I give an invitation, I mean it. If you cared for new things, I should have been afraid to ask you; but if you really like what is musty, why there's no more to be said; and you will have in my old owl's nest a musty old woman into the bargain.'

"'If you wish me to stay with you,' I said, 'till you even suggest what you call yourself, you would have to keep me for the term of my natural life.'

"'Nonsense,' she answered, 'I don't want compliments. I want to know if you are going to do what I ask you. I go home to-morrow myself; and if you will arrive next day, a well-aired bed will be ready for you, and the fire in the parlor lighted. So come—decide upon coming, and stay as long as you can amuse yourself.

"The invitation was so unexpected, and I was so delighted with it, that I could at first hardly believe her serious. But I soon saw that she was. My evident pleasure pleased her; and without more ado we proceeded to trains and routes. The journey is easy enough. There is a station near the castle; and going one way one can reach it in ten hours; going another, one must sleep a night on the road. 'The last way,' she said, 'was by far the most interesting, as it takes one through a beautiful part of Styria.' I therefore selected that. I shall accordingly start the day after to-morrow, and the day after that I shall arrive at this mysterious castle. Five years ago I know one thing I should have done—I should have occupied the intervening day with calling on Lady Ashford—not for the sake of resuming my discussion with her, but of gratifying my curiosity by a further acquaintance with her niece. But now such a prospect is hardly even a temptation to me; though, perhaps, if the niece were before me, its force would be just appreciable.

"Well! so in a few days I shall be in the heart of a strange country—and a country how strange! how interesting! It is a country which always has haunted my imagination, owing to the fragments of description which from time to time I had heard of it. It is a country still of overgrown feudal households where the retainers loyally kiss the hands of their masters; where bears and wild boars roam in forests, whose alleys are watched by keepers in plumed hats, and in whose recesses brigands hide themselves; where tribes of gypsies wander, and where gypsy bands play. It is a country which no doubt has known a political revolution, but no social revolution, or at the utmost only the shadow of one. Here is [the past living still in the present.] One crosses a Rubicon, and goes back a hundred and fifty years. Of course, to a certain extent, I write all this at random: the only Hungary that I know is the Hungary that I imagine. But I do not think, anyhòw, I am wrong in expecting this—to inhale an atmosphere scented with the life of another century. Will not that be romance, as I said just now? Will it?

"Sleep—you are coming at last to me. I am coming to you, to pillow myself among happy prospects."

CHAPTER III.

It was nearly one o'clock when Grenville laid down his pen. At the same hour, two nights later, he was in a very different situation. His servant Fritz, an Austrian, who knew the country thoroughly, and to whom he committed the entire management of his journey, had just roused him up and extracted him from the drowsy twilight of a railway carriage—extracted him into a gust of night wind vaguely scented, and escorted him with his rugs and dressing-bags into the refreshment room of some unknown junction.

"Our train," said Fritz, "does not go for an hour. Perhaps, excellency, you will allow me to order a little supper for you. See," he said, taking a list of refreshments from a table, "this soup is good—you get it never in Vienna; these sausages are good; and this wine—you should taste that."

Partly by way of getting rid of the time, partly by way of acknowledging his servant's care for him, Grenville let the supper be ordered, and sat down to wait for it. Half awake as he was, the scene seemed like a dream to him. The air was hazy with gas-lit filaments of tobacco smoke; odd looking men with peaked caps and spectacles were beguiling their minutes with beer at little marble tables, while their luggage, mostly in the shape of miniature canvas pormanteaus, lay at their feet like dogs. Muffled women with bundles came and went, or sat wearily on red velvet benches. Coffee machines with great brass domes gleamed at a long counter, and the walls, lined with pitch-pine, made a bare background for everything, checkered with advertisements of unfamiliar liqueurs and drinks. The whole place was charged with a sense of nocturnal traveling—of a fragment of active life strayed into the regions of sleep.

Grenville ate his supper with curiosity rather than appetite, and then went out and smoked his cigar upon the platform. Near, in a valley, were the street lights of some silent town; to the right and left were the scattered station buildings—masses of shadow starred with a colored lamp or two; and all around were hills covered with pine forests, which showed in the dim moonlight their serrated outlines against the sky. Grenville was ignorant of the name, and even of the locality, of the station. All the country round was steeped in the charm of mystery. By and by some figures issued from the refreshment-room, crossing the rails to another platform beyond; and before long, with a rumbling moan out of the silence, came a lighted passenger train, sliding and hissing, and arresting itself. A few moments more, and it has passed away like a somnambulist. Grenville looked at his watch, and his servant's voice at his ear said, "Our train next. It comes here in five minutes. Here, excellency, is the station master. He will keep a compartment, if he can, for you. I know him. His father was steward to the last Prince Plekonitz."

Grenville turned round, and acknowledged the profound bow of a functionary, whose gold braid glittered and whose whiskers shivered with authority. A whistle pierced the night; there was another rumbling moan;

and presently close to the group a procession of lighted windows, and shining sides of carriages bearing the word "Trieste" on them, moved and became stationary. The station master was as good as his word. With much ceremony, after a little talk with the guard, he bowed Grenville into a reserved compartment, saying to the former as he did so, "His excellency alights at G——. Your excellency will arrive there at half-past four in the morning."

"Certainly," said Grenville, smiling to himself, as he stretched himself out on the cushions, "I am an exception to the rule that no man is a hero to his valet. Fritz imagines me a minister of state already; and what is even more to the purpose, he communicates his own conception of me to his friends." The truth of this reflection was experienced even at G——, when in the chill obscurity of the station a commissionaire from the hotel, who had been joined by the guard the moment the train arrived, appeared at the door of the compartment, and assisted his excellency to descend. In these days everything has to be paid for; the bow of the departing guard indicated that he had been paid sufficiently; and Grenville before long, in a heavy rattling omnibus, was being shaken to pieces over the paving stones of a dim angular street. After lasting for ten minutes, this torture came to an end, and the vehicle halted abruptly under a huge resonant archway. Some men with lanterns emerged from a glass door; within one belated gas-jet gleamed on some stone stairs; and Grenville presently, in an atmosphere of ghostly quiet, was passing to his room by the gallery of a frescoed hall, one side of which was covered with a coat-of-arms, and bore the date of 1620. "This inn, sir," said Fritz, as he opened his master's door, "is very old—more than two hundred years." And so it well might be, thought Grenville as he closed his eyes. Already, into the present, it seemed to his imagination that the past had projected a long fantastic shadow.

The dreams of sleep are killed by a bright morning. The dreams of our waking life take often a new vigor from it. So, next morning, for Grenville, a thousand new fancies, all of them children of the same waking dreamland, came floating into his rooms as Fritz opened the windows, and admitted, in doing so, a breath of that faint unfamiliar smell which whispers to a stranger's nerves the news that he is in a strange city. As for G——, it is no doubt perfectly true that many an Englishman might roam through every street of it and be struck by nothing in any of them, excepting its inferiority to Bayswater; but the minds of some men, if not their eyes, are color blind. To Grenville the very names of the shops, the conformation of the roofs and chimneys, and even the shape of the primitive cart wheels, were things which touched his imagination as a breeze touches the sea, and made it shiver into some new colors. Fritz was his guide for an hour or so, and did the honors of the place for him. By the middle of the day he was once more in the train, and was speeding away from roofs and streets and chimneys, and piercing the country, beyond whose borders was Hungary.

And now, indeed, a duller imagination than his might have found excitement in the scenes which were pouring past him. All the backgrounds of all the romances of the world seemed to him to be suddenly turning into realities; or else nature itself seemed to be turning unreal, and to be receiving him into a universe of illusions.] These mountains covered with interminable forests, these green winding valleys, with tiled hamlets gleaming in them, these deeply rutted roads flanked with wayside crosses, these water-mills with the Middle Ages clinging to their cumbrous wheels—pictures of this kind each seen for a minute or two, and vivified now and then by bright-colored rustic figures, came to Grenville all with a delightful magic about them—with an enchanted music like the overture to some new experience. Who has not at times, when traveling even in his own country, known some feeling similar? Who, catching sight, through the moving windows of the railway carriage, of some old orieled manor house, half hidden among its avenues, has not seen in it the casket of some inaccessible novel, and imputed some breath of love to the slopes where the deer wander? And if this can be felt at home in our own modernized England, how would the feeling not be quickened in Styria—a land where the following vision presently startled Grenville? An isolated rock, some thousand feet in height, scarred with precipices and fledged with enormous pines, among which gleamed an ascending line of towers, while crowning the summit was a castle spiked with pinnacles. Within view of this spectacle was a little wayside station at which the train stopped; so Grenville was able to assure himself that what he looked at really existed. The whole structure seemed perfect. Glass gleamed in the windows. The train moved on and his eyes became more expectant. By and by, nearer the line, a hunting-lodge peeped out of the forest, with a great black coronet daubed on its white plaster; then, far off, like a ship's masts on the horizon, one or two towers rose above a sea of pine trees; then came a station, near to a red-roofed town, whose gray fortifications were marked by a line of lindens; and then another castle, half lost in a park, with fanciful Grecian temples scattered among the foliage.

At last, however, the aspect of things changed. The mountains died away into long low-lying slopes; and soon the train was moving in a sea-like expanse of plain. Now and again came some sloping uplands, on the ridge of one of which a castle or country house was seen distending itself, like a great bleached barrack; but these were left behind, and presently there was nothing but flatness, edged at the remotest skyline by low, faint hills, cobalt-colored. At first this transition tended to disappoint Grenville. Huge parallelograms of plow land, alternating with waste and pasture, chilled his fancy with homely reminiscences of Lincolnshire; but by and by his eyes came to be conscious of various strange details, which once more enchanted everything. The names of the stations had become uncouth and alien; the words on the doors of the waiting-rooms and the offices were in an un-European language, suggesting no conjecturable meaning. Here and there on the plain, watching his wandering charge, was some solitary shepherd, or swineherd, grasping his long crook, and loosely covered with a capote of Oriental fashion; while above the roofs of villages islanded in sprouting orchards, the towers of the churches showed themselves with bulging Oriental domes. Grenville now knew where he was. Everything spoke of Hungary.

So the hours wore on, the prospect hardly changing itself, till at last the traveler, thrusting his head out of the window, descried in the distance a new distinguishing feature—an enormous poplar avenue straight as a line, crossing the whole landscape, and disappearing on each horizon. Watching this with a vague feeling of curiosity, he saw the trees grow more and more distinct; soon, between them and him, a small town showed itself —a church, some rows of houses, and the chimney of one engine-house. Passing these, the train slacked its speed, and then stopped with a jerk at a dwarfed, disconsolate station. Here, among a group of farmers and earth-stained peasants, was a figure whose presence distinguished this station from all the others—the figure of a footman, having a red cockade in his hat, and a long well-made overcoat, bright with immense gilt buttons. In a moment Fritz appeared at the carriage door; and Grenville knew the journey was all but ended.

Outside the gate were waiting a spruce-looking brougham and a high outlandish break, with some wild-eyed gypsies staring at them. Grenville was presently at home among the civilized cushions of the former; and the horses, at the sound of the whip, plunged forward impetuously. One incongruous sensation at once surprised and amused him, and that was the rocking and jolting of the eminently well-hung vehicle, which told a refreshing tale of the savage character of the road. In a few minutes a sharp turn was taken, and then he saw he was in the great poplar avenue. On each side was a deep irregular ditch, beyond were glimpses of tiled barns and cottages, and ahead of him, in the distance, it seemed that the road was blocked by some vague masses of building, on which something or other glittered. In due time all this explained itself. The brougham was approaching a long buff-colored wall, built of stone elaborately dressed, and enriched with ciphers at intervals; and in the middle of this was a florid Italian gateway, high over which was lifted a gilded princely coronet. Some doors were opened, a man in a green livery raised a hat full of plumes to the carriage; gravel crunched under the wheels; some barefooted women were visible, grubbing in unkempt flower beds; then came shadow and echo, and the horses tramped under an archway; they crossed a well-like court surrounded by walls and windows, and drew up under a second archway beyond. Here on a step was standing a majestic porter, with gold lace on his coat and a gold-headed staff of office in his hand. Through the door behind him was visible a great ascending staircase, on which were stationed several liveried servants, a wizened little dwarf, who might have been either sixteen or sixty, and a steward who would have done honor to any German melodrama, as he smiled and blinked a respectful benediction on the scene. Grenville feared for a moment that they would all of them be kissing his hand—an act which, though he approved of it in theory, would, he felt, be embarrassing in practice. As a matter of fact, however, they merely muttered something and bowed; and somehow or other between them conducted him up the staircase. This was not unlike the staircase of a palace at Genoa. There was the same spaciousness, the same fine proportions, though the stairs and balustrades were of coarse stone, not marble, and the walls were rudely whitewashed. But a life-size portrait of Maria Theresa was on one side, a cardinal simpered superb benevolence on the other; and facing the landing was a wigged general under a canopy, turning a velvet shoulder to an army being massacred in the background. Grenville found at this point that the dwarf alone was conducting him. He was ushered through two bare anterooms, whose walls were dingy with pictures. A farther door was opened. He heard a voice that he recognized; and the Princess, full of smiles, was greeting him in a good-sized drawing-room. Here everything had an oddly familiar look—tables, carpet, and sofas. It all suggested England—only an England just robbed of its comfort. There was English comfort, however, in the sight of the tea-table ready for him; and he and the Princess were soon happily seated with nothing between them but a service of old Vienna china.

"You mustn't be frightened," she said, "at finding me quite alone. Some time next week there will be a few people coming—Count C——, perhaps, who was once Ambassador in London; and a nice little niece of mine with two angels of children. To-night, too, at dinner, I have company for you in the shape of the priest. He talks nothing but Hungarian, so I must be his interpreter. Poor man—this will make his conversation go further than usual. You see," she went on, "I have taken you at your word; and you will have nothing to amuse you here but the things you told me you cared about—a half-civilized country which is strange to you, and an old draughty castle, where I hope you are already at home. Hark!" she exclaimed sharply, "I believe I hear my grandchildren. If it's not too dark to see, come outside and look at them."

He opened a window for her, and they emerged on the leaded roof of a portico. Below was an enormous court, inclosed symmetrically by out-buildings, and having in the middle a grass plot, which encircled a towering obelisk.

"Ah," said the Princess, "my beauties! Look at them, there they are—all waddling up to the old Prince Ludwig's monument."

Grenville's eye followed the direction of hers; and thus guided he discovered a flock of turkeys straying about at will as if the whole place were a farmyard.

"Look! look!" said the Princess, smiling at them through her spectacles. "That's Tommy and that's Francis Joseph. Don't you like my grandchildren? And there behind that grand gate are my great-nephews and great-nieces, the pigs. Ain't I foolish?" she went on as she turned away. "I live so much alone that my fancies are my companions."

Grenville meanwhile had been contemplating the poplar avenue whose slim vista reached away into the twilight beyond an entrance opposite to him that was guarded by two great statues. "That avenue," said the Princess, "was made by my husband's grandfather, to form a link between two distant properties. In that direction it goes for more than sixty miles, and sixteen in the other; and this castle is stuck on it like a piece of meat on a skewer. How dark it is getting! but still, I can tell you a little of our geography. On one side of us is our town—you would call it a village; on the other the park, into which your bedroom looks; and north and south are our poplars and open country. That great building is a riding-school; the other that faces it is a ballroom; and those two things like temples to the right and left of the entrance, coachmen and gardeners live now in them; but forty years back they were the quarters of a guard of honor. Yes," she said, looking at him with an amused twinkle in her eyes, "we have only just ceased to be interesting savages. I hope you'll discover to-morrow that we're not quite civilized yet. Hark, that bell means it is half-past six. We dine at seven. I will have you shown to your room. Don't dress; put on merely a morning coat; and listen—one piece of advice; take your hat with you and wear it in these cold passages."

The dwarf, who was found in the anteroom, and who seemed a kind of groom of the chambers, actually had Grenville's hat ready for him; and guiding him down the stairs to a vaulted corridor on an entresol, landed him at last in a bedroom that was vaulted also, though the curves of the roof, as well as the walls, were incongruously covered with a cheap English paper. Having made the toilette enjoined him, Grenville retraced his steps, and found the Princess and the priest already waiting him in the drawing-room. The priest rose deferentially and, with both hands on his stomach, made a bend of the body toward him with a smile interpreted as a bow. The Princess rattled through a bilingual introduction, and then said, "Take your hats, and let us come in to dinner." They passed out through the anteroom, across the head of the staircase, and presently reached a large circular chamber, rudely frescoed, so as to look like a ruinous temple, with a broken dome for its roof, and ferns sprouting out of its wall.

Compared with an English dinner the repast was primitively simple. The dishes were few, and each was presented twice; there was nothing on the table but a dish of pears, and biscuits; and there was one wine only—a red wine of the country. To Grenville, fresh from the luxuries of Vienna and London, all this seemed like a happy retrogression into shadow-land; and the number of clumsily reverential servants who shuffled round so bare a board, deepened this vague impression. A mere accident deepened it yet further. The Princess worked industriously as interpreter between the priest and Grenville; but presently Grenville, feeling that he cut rather a helpless figure, asked if the priest was able to talk Latin. The good man's face at once lighted up, and a smile widened the curve of his smooth overflowing cheeks. With his knife arrested an inch in front of his mouth, he emitted first a cough, and then a few halting words, which Grenville barely recognized through their unaccustomed pronunciation; but to which, however, he bravely responded by some others, imitating as well as he could the pronunciation of his neighbor. In the course of a few minutes the two began just to understand each other. As time went on they got more shameless and confident, and gradually casting to the winds all reverence for grammatical virtue, they became intelligible as they ceased to attempt correctness. The Princess was delighted. She asked in Hungarian and English what they were saying, and by and by she was informed that they had got on the subject of the castle. The castle to the priest was the most magnificent object in the universe; and he evidently felt a kind of personal pride in recounting to a stranger all the wonders contained in it. Moreover as this kind of catalogue obviated the necessity for verbs, he continued it in the drawing-room till the early hour arrived for him and his cassock to bow themselves out and vanish. "Theatrum

—scena—proscenium—" these were some of the echoes left by him in his listener's ears—"arma cum multis gemmis—arma antiquissima—documenta—libri—medii ævi reliquiæ—mirabilia multa—permulta—admiranda! Sylvæ—cervi—latifundia prodigiosa."

CHAPTER IV.

THE expectations which Grenville took that night to bed with him, were well fulfilled by the experience of the following week; and the hush that pervaded the place owing to the absence of company, left him full leisure to appreciate the new impressions that were invading him. He woke each morning in his arched chamber to find his coffee at his bedside, in exquisite old pink china. He looked from the window on the giant trees of the park—a park planted after the fashion of regal France, in long alleys that radiated from an open space in the center. When his window was open, there would come an influx of air which had all the warmth of summer, and all the odor of spring; and he would steal out early down a narrow winding staircase, and wander at will among the huge trunks and the primroses, treading on moss, and watching the roofs and outlines of the castle. Wherever he turned was something with the stamp of *ancienna régime* on it. There was a long orangery built in the seventeenth century; a kitchen garden with forcing houses hardly later in date; and as to the castle itself, its newest parts or features—the great courtyard which was meant to be grandly classical—some Corinthian pilasters stuck against mediæval walls, and some Italian vases stuck on mediæval parapets—these were the work of a lady, not a Princess Plekonitz, whom a Prince Plekonitz had imported here from the court of

Louis Quatorze. Grenville each morning saw them all with the dew on them; while on every side of him, the innumerable buds of spring swelled and brightened into one growing illumination of green.

Then, too, within doors the castle unfolded its details. He came upon rows of pictures painted with rude force, representing wars on the Turkish border, and full of burning towns, falling flags with the crescent on them, and savage turbaned heads being severed by Hungarian sabers. The old steward lured him up many dusty stairs, and introduced him to a veritable museum hidden in the topmost story. Here were whitewashed walls, festooned with jeweled saddle cloths of crimson and green velvet—the plunder of Moslem camps. In one room were antique saddles, of which some had emeralds in their stirrups; in another was battered armor, and great rusty lances; in another matchlocks and models of old artillery; and in another a pile of faded Turkish pavilions. Then, again, under rafters that smelt of cobwebs, were worm-eaten presses whose contents exhaled a different sentiment—dies for money, which the princes once had the right of coining; toys of forgotten children; rapiers with tarnished handles, rouge-pots, velvet masks, and fragments of broken fans—withered petals of the gayety of a lost century. Again, there were ponderous quaint portmanteaus, which had rumbled their last on wheels before the French Revolution; a chest, with a service in it of metal plates and dishes, for the use of some prince when he halted at wayside inns—objects which whispered of coaches with blazoned panels, armed retinues, and long robber-haunted roads. Nor was the priest's boast a vain one when he spoke of old documents, and of a theater. There was in the basement a series of vaulted chambers, stacked with papers and parchments, like trusses of brown hay, which made Grenville feel as if all the past were breathing at him; and above the drawing-room was a high saloon full of silence, where a regular stage stood with all its scenery, in the same condition as when actors had last trodden it, on a certain gay festival ninety years ago.

He had little temptation at first to wander beyond the precincts, the castle and its grounds offering quite enough to amuse him; but occasional glimpses which he caught of the outer world made a fitting frame for the things with which he had grown familiar. The windows of the library commanded the square of the little town, which the second day of his visit was thronged with a many-colored fair, the whole area being tesselated with the costumes of peasants and gypsies. A day or two later he saw the same open space perambulated by a procession bearing tapers, crosses, and censers, and led by chanting priests, whose vestments twinkled in the daylight: and beyond the fences of the park he gradually came to realize there were plains where buffaloes fed, and—better still than this—where sheep wandered, with shepherds playing on pastoral pipes to them.

The Princess, who had lived so long in her adopted country that anything strange about it had by this time worn away, began to feel, when her guest described his experiences to her, that she saw it with fresh eyes again, and her interest in it was revived by his. The nights were so warm that, leaving the lighted drawing-room, they sat outside on the roof of the portico after dinner, talking of the life surrounding them—talking of the robbers that still haunted the country, of the powers still exercised by some of the rural magnates and of romantic stories and legends of this and of that family; and she sometimes alluded to a possession of the house of Plekonitz, which she said that Grenville ought by and by to see—a half-ruined castle on a rock, some sixteen miles away, with quarters in it for a thousand troops; and a hall, like a brick cathedral, called "the hall of the canon." And meanwhile, from a tavern beyond the lodges would float, with a dreamy wildness, the music of a gypsy band; the moon, rising above the blossoming horse chestnuts of the park, would make in their branches a mist of milky lamplight, and out of the thickets beyond would thrill the first notes of the nightingale.

But at last came a day of rain; and he then betook himself to a region which he had as yet quite neglected—the library. The bulk of the books were French—books of the last century, and many of them were extremely curious. There were quaint guides to old-world watering places; quaint treatises on old-world household economy; and others, without number, on building, containing plans and pictures of mansions in the Faubourg St. Germain, and of châteaux in the days of their glory. In addition to these he found a collection of tall folios, which were full of superb engravings, illustrating, in the most minute way, the life of Paris and Vienna, from the street to the royal bedroom.

These the Princess had never seen before, and her pleasure in them knew no bounds. She and Grenville, before they went to bed, would spend an hour in turning them over like children. Brilliant balls, banquets, and royal card-parties, fanciful outdoor fêtes, hunting scenes, and processions, all drawn from life with the most exact minuteness, were revealed before them on the splendid unwieldy pages. The gilded chariots seemed to rattle as they looked at them, the flowers to be sprouting in the alleys of the grandiose gardens, and they heard on the towering hedges the clink of the gardener's shears. But Grenville at last discovered something better even than this. It was a little oblong volume in tattered and dirty calf, which he chanced to unearth, and opened it with very faint curiosity. But when he opened it he found it the identical thing which he had wished for secretly, without imagining it existed. It was a collection of engravings published two hundred years ago, of the castles of Hungary and Styria, showing them as they then were. The superb folios at once ceased to interest him, and his imagination gave itself entirely to these strange romantic dwellings. Some were perched on curious rocks like bird's nests, some hung with their turrets over little clustering villages, some stood in great woodlands, solitary. But all had the same peculiar air about them, distinct from anything known to Western Europe. They were all of them mansions or palaces incorporated with the feudal stronghold, not as if this last were the work of a dead antiquity, but as being obviously a part of the real life of the time. There were Italian gardens hidden behind cannon and watch towers, Italian gateways flanked by walls loopholed for musketry, and traveling carriages issuing out under the teeth of the raised portcullis.

And now came the question, where were these castles situated? And which of these, if any, could Grenville manage to visit? The Princess understood his enthusiasm, but she could give him little information. She accordingly sent for an agent who managed part of the property; she submitted the book to him, and catechized him carefully as to its contents. Of many of the castles he naturally knew nothing; but a dozen or more, belonging to the adjacent region, he at once identified, and could say something about them. Of these several he knew to be complete ruins, but three or four of them—and they happened to be among the most singular—he said were standing much as the pictures showed them, and he engaged to find out how they might best be visited.

One excursion, indeed, was arranged at once, and that was to the castle of which the Princess had herself spoken. A light carriage and four were put at Grenville's disposal. Early one morning the horses stamped under the archway, the porter in his gold lace and his robes superintended the start, and past the lodges, and beneath the glittering coronet, Grenville sped away into the level limitless landscape, inhaling the smell and freshness of the half Oriental spring. He came back in the evening enchanted with what he had seen. Everything had deepened in him the odd sense of primitiveness which he had received at the windows of the railway carriage. Everything had spoken of a world that was lost to Western Europe—the peasants who lifted their shaggy caps as he passed; the tracts of forest through which the road had taken him, where gypsy bands camped in clearings, and woodmen on the borders of the shadow were cutting the raw red timber; and above all the aspect of the villages. These were the same, in every typical feature, as those drawn in the old volume of castles; while, as for the village at the foot of the castle he was bound for, the moment he came in sight of it he had recognized all the houses. The castle itself he had found to be more than half a ruin, but in other respects it had astonished him. The sides of the rock which it occupied were encrusted with prisons and guard-rooms: he had reached the summit through a line of ascending towers, whose iron doors swung in the breezy shadow; he had found a labyrinth of great subterranean galleries; beyond a grass-grown yard that was littered with rusty cannon, he had come on a tower full of portraits and crystal goblets; and perched in the air over the nave of a lofty chapel was a banqueting hall, complete with accessories that might have walked straight out of Wardour Street—armor and arms, and worm-eaten black sideboards, and a long oak table surrounded by carved chairs.

"Well," said the Princess, at dinner, "I can tell you some good news. The agent has been here to-day with me, and he has arranged two more expeditions for you— to castles that are as large as this one—and he says not ruined at all. To see these, however, you must sleep for a couple of nights at a little town about thirty miles away: so as one or two people are almost directly coming here, you had better, perhaps, calm your impatience and wait until they are gone. Remember," she added, "there are my little great-nieces and their mother. For my sake you must stay and admire these; and then, as I told you, there also will be Count C——. He knows Hungary thoroughly, and he was for some years at Constantinople, so for every reason you ought to be here to meet him."

"Nothing," said Grenville, "could please me, or suit me, better. I have letters to answer, and many matters to think over; and, until your guests come, I shall really be glad of quiet."

CHAPTER V.

QUIET, indeed, he welcomed for many reasons. His imagination, he found, was being touched by the life about him to a degree he had never expected. He had told Lady Ashford he felt it as good as dead; and here, a week later, it was actually turning him into a boy again. Of this he was made more conscious than ever, the following day, when he set himself to answer his letters. They had been forwarded from the Embassy at Vienna—a big formidable packet. The tone of them all, as well as the matter, was flattering; and they flushed his mind with the sense that he was really a rising man. And yet as he sat at the window of his vaulted bedroom, writing his clear answers to them, and feeling his power in doing so, the thought of his surroundings would constantly touch his nerves like a perfume—a delightful consciousness of the castle, with its ancient passages, of the Turkish spoils, the rouge pots, the velvet masks—of the primitive villages, the forests, and the great pastoral plains. All appealed to him like a wild breath of romance; and romance seemed a more attractive thing than reality. He enjoyed the sensation, but at first he was somewhat alarmed at it; and he welcomed a quiet which would allow him to examine his symptoms. He asked himself whether, after all, he were not merely a dreamer, and whether he were not already tiring of his new career. "To succeed," he said to himself, "what one wants is will. Is not my will once more being drugged or seduced by my imagination?" But he soon convinced himself that such an alarm was groundless. The impersonal romance which was charming him, he reflected very justly, unlike devotion to a woman, was no rival to ambition; indeed, as that night he explained at length in his diary, its tendency rather was to make his ambition keener.

"All work in the world," he wrote, "except religious work, among its motives has always ambition for one of them; and if anyone says this is not true in his own case, it merely means that his ambition is a kind of ambition he is ashamed of. Now ambition is essentially an appreciation of some prize that the world can give one: and nothing depraves ambition, and in my own case deadens it, so much as the sense, which one cannot escape in England, of how the world's prizes are being affected by the growth of the democratic spirit. It is only when the constitution of society is openly and avowedly aristocratic that ambition can be gentlemanly, or even honest. An ambitious democrat is bound to achieve his elevation by making a trade of saying he does not wish to be elevated; and then, when he does achieve it, what a ridiculous elevation it is. He is like a man chaired by a mob, and every moment in danger of being upset by it. But in this country, so far at least as a stranger sees, there are neither mobs nor democrats. This castle, were it in England, would no doubt seem rude and uncomfortable: but its towers and courtyards have here nothing to rival them: and it is just in the same way here that the spirit of aristocracy survives, not really, perhaps, with more vigor than in England, but with nothing, so far as a stranger sees, to question it. One feels it here as one does not feel it there. It forms quietly a kind of atmosphere round one; it restores to life a lost picturesqueness and brilliance; and it makes the world a place that seems better worth succeeding in."

If these impressions were strong when he wrote them down, they were destined the following day to be strengthened still further. The Princess announced at luncheon, with a certain air of importance, that the Count and Countess were coming that afternoon. "Irma Schilizzi," she added, "has put me off till to-morrow." Then she paused. "The Count and Countess," she resumed presently, "as of course you know, are among the greatest—the very greatest—people in Vienna. It's a pity you never met them. They were in London before your time."

Grenville noticed in her manner a certain touch of nervousness. With some surprise he presently saw the cause of it.

"The Count and I," continued the Princess, "are very old friends. We always get on famously. As for her, her manners can be perfectly charming; and here she'll of course be civil. But——"

"Well," said Grenville, "but what?"

The Princess gave a little laugh. "You don't know Vienna," she said. "Well, no more do I. I never tried to do so. Shall I explain why to you? Listen to me. You see what I am—the widow of the greatest magnate in Hungary; and foreigner though I am, I can tell you that at Buda-Pesth I am as great a lady as anyone—perhaps I am even the greatest. But at Vienna I shouldn't be so much as received in society. My mother belonged to one of the oldest families in England. Her mother was the daughter of an English duke; but my father and his father were brewers—only merchant princes and liberal statesmen. And at Vienna—I tell you I'm not exaggerating—I should be nobody—nobody—nobody. These Austrian countesses and princesses—well, there's no use talking about it. As you didn't know this one in London, see how she treats *you*. I thought till this morning that he would be here without her: but she's on her way to some place, so she makes this house a convenience."

One of these observations slightly annoyed Grenville. The Countess might have a contempt for brewers and brewers' children, but he saw no reason why he should be classed along with them. He not only, however, was careful to hide this feeling, but he resolved that, no matter how the Countess treated him, he would pretend that she had kept him at a distance, and so share the lot of his hostess. He saw the subject was a sore one with her, though she had herself started it, so he said abruptly, by way of turning the conversation:

"And who is Irma Schilizzi, who you said is coming to-morrow?"

"My niece—my niece," said the Princess, a little impatiently. "I suppose I am stupid, and didn't tell you her name. There is a case in point. She lives in Vienna sometimes. Her husband has business there. He is one of a firm of engineers. He is very rich; he has done some great works for the Emperor; and so his name is perfectly well known. As for getting into Viennese society, my niece would as soon think of trying to get to the moon. But to her the Countess will be not only civil but charming. She considers the distance between them to be so immense and acknowledged, that she will be almost as nice to her as she might be to a favorite maid. These people—I tell you you'll be able to see it for yourself—can be charming to those whom they acknowledge their equals, and also to those who acknowledge themselves their inferiors; but to others, their insolence is something that an Englishwoman could hardly believe in. It's all the greater, because they hardly seem to be aware of it. Not that I care," she added, with true feminine veracity. "Perhaps she'll amuse you. She's a handsome woman, but very stupid."

This formidable lady and her husband arrived about five o'clock. Entering the drawing-room Grenville found them at tea; and after all he had heard he watched them with some interest. The Count, a handsome man, who looked about sixty-five, with his frank expression and carefully trimmed beard, had all the air of a high-bred fashionable Englishman. The Countess was a slim woman, who had many remains of beauty, and evidently a Parisian maid, and she was prattling to the Princess with all the lightness of a girl, in a quick alternation of German, French, and English. The Count, as Grenville had expected, greeted him with great cordiality, but he was completely surprised at meeting the same reception from her. She turned toward him with a bright twinkle of welcome, which seemed to come at once from her eyes, her lips, and her jewelry. "Mr. Grenville," she said, in the prettiest foreign accent, "I didn't know we were going to find you here. We were so sorry, the Count and I, not to have met you at Vienna. Dear

Princess, let Mr. Grenville sit by me. Perhaps you'll allow him just to move the tea table."

Grenville experienced two conflicting emotions. He would hardly have been human if he had not felt somewhat flattered at being distinguished thus by a lady whom he had been told he would find so *difficile*. But another emotion, which he was far more keenly conscious of, was annoyance for the sake of the Princess, who he felt, in spite of her kindness, would be mortified for several reasons at this falsification of her prophecies. He honestly wished that the Countess would begin to be rude to him; he did as little as possible to meet her friendly advances; and he carefully kept from looking toward the Princess, for fear she should think he was asking her to remark his conquest. By and by, however, the Countess suddenly said to him, "And Mr. Grenville, how beautiful they are, those poems of yours! Your Ambassador lent them to me. I think there is real passion in them."

Grenville's eyes, in modesty, wandered away from the speaker, and they fell by accident full on those of the Princess. He was puzzled by seeing in them no signs of annoyance, but a knowing smile which said to him, "Isn't it as I told you?" What she could mean by this he was quite unable to conjecture: but the moment the Count and Countess were taken to see their bedrooms, she explained it by saying to him, with a little friendly malice, "Don't you notice how she takes you for a man of letters, and patronizes you?"

"Well," said Grenville, with a really generous effort, "perhaps she does. I confess I did feel patronized."

Never was lie told with a more successful charity. The Princess laughed, delighted, and rubbed her hands together. "Ah," she said, "didn't I tell you so? That's Vienna all over."

Grenville was satisfied that he had wiped out the mischief; but, as fate would have it, at dinner it all began again. The conversation turned at first on various royal marriages, and then on the general gossip of half the courts of Europe. Nothing in the world could have suited the Princess better. Of Rome and St. Petersburg she knew far more than the Countess, and despite her opinion of the Austrian *haute noblesse*, she had the *Almanach de Gotha* well at her fingers' ends. Then presently, when the Countess, who loved jewelry like a child, said to her, "Oh, *mon Dieu*, what a beautiful brooch that is of yours!" she achieved a genuine triumph in being able to answer thus: "The Queen of England gave it me. She was fond of me for the sake of my grandmother."

"Yes," said the Count to his wife, anxious to make things pleasant, "the Princess was always a great favorite with the Queen."

"I know England so little," said the Countess, turning to Grenville. "I only married my husband during his last year in London. I stayed one autumn, however, at several of your beautiful châteaux. Compared with you English we poor people are barbarous."

"On the contrary," said Grenville, "I hear your châteaux are splendid. Your country life has always particularly interested me."

The Princess, who thought that Grenville still felt patronized, was anxious now to speak up for his dignity.

"Mr. Grenville," she interposed, "has a beautiful old château of his own."

"Ah," said the Countess, laughing gayly, "to be sure he has. We have been there, we have seen it. We were staying with Lord Solway, and he drove us through the enchanting park. You don't live there? No? I was told it was let to some rich *bourgeois*. But we went in. We saw all of your old pictures, and one—I recognized one—of a lady I know well. Your aunt, I suppose she is, Countess Juliet Grenville, the *Chanoinesse*. So you see we know all about you; and your Ambassador said at Vienna you will be such a great man. You ought to be great," she went on, with an almost coquettish friendliness. "I am not laughing—no. It is written in your eyes. I am a physiognomist."

Grenville felt that the Princess was taking in every word: and later in the evening he hoped she was out of hearing, when the Count, who treated him with equally marked distinction, offered to give him this and that introduction to obnoxious grandees, the despisers of brewers' daughters, in case he should really wish to see country life in Austria. The Princess, however, had managed to hear everything; but she was far too genial and dignified to feel any real annoyance at it: and she only indulged in the solace, which an angel could hardly have grudged her, of trying to make it appear that everything had happened as she predicted.

"Did you notice?" she said. "They treat you as one of themselves. You see the reason. They happen to know your pedigree—I daresay better than you know it yourself. Isn't it just as I told you? Only I never thought it would have come out so soon. Well, the

Countess is satisfied that your blood is blue. She never forgets that mine has malt and hops in it."

"My dear Princess," said Grenville, "I'm sure you are wrong there. This lady seems to treat you as her intimate friend."

"Stuff!" said the Princess, laughing, as she said goodnight to him. "You don't understand women. Civility with a fine lady is often the grammar of impertinence."

The whole of these incidents somewhat jarred upon Grenville. He was sorry for his hostess, whose life, for the next few days would, he saw, be ruffled by some old sense of indignity; but he was annoyed at having had her grievance confided to himself. It seemed like a breath of common and incongruous prose, disenchanting the air of his lonely and princely castle. In this mood of mind the society of the Count and Countess gave him a pleasure by contrast, which he could not help feeling, but for which he reproached himself as if it savored of treachery. There was a soothing calm about them, especially in their social judgments, which said that for them a social grievance would be impossible. They also showed not only perfect taste, but the kindness that comes to people for whom acrimony could never be a necessity. In the Count, too, he noticed a certain chivalrous discrimination, when he mentioned the Princess's niece—a mere *bourgeois*, the wife of an engineer.

"We met her here," he said, "last year—a pretty, refined woman."

"Yes," said the Countess carelessly; "her mother, I think, was noble."

"You would quite get the impression," the Count continued to Grenville, "that she had made a *mésalliance* in marrying this Schilizzi—a Levantine. He's rich—he must be; and has a great villa at Hampstead. Some day in London you'll be making a fashionable man of him."

In these last words was a dryness that spoke volumes. Soon afterward the Countess, with a pleasant smile, happened to say of the Princess, "So clever, so nice, so good she is." These words spoke their volumes also. Grenville now detected the note of instinctive patronage, and was certainly not displeased that he was not himself its victim. The sense that he was not—the sense that these two fastidious aristocrats, while patronizing others, saw in himself an equal, gave him in his own eyes a certain increased importance, the very nature of which he would hardly have understood at home, or which at home he would certainly have thought ridiculous. He was indeed conscious of something ridiculous in it even here. Still it was a stimulant; it lifted him up and braced him; and the fame and brilliant position that promised to be the reward of his exertions seemed not only more necessary to him, but more nearly in his grasp than ever.

But presently an incident happened which disturbed his mood, and made him despise himself for indulging in it. Mrs. Schilizzi arrived—a clear-eyed, graceful blonde, somewhat timid in manners, but perfectly well-bred. Grenville was by instinct always attentive to women, even to those who appealed to nothing beyond his kindness. And here was a woman to whom, under other circumstances, he would certainly have found it pleasant to pay some common attention. Indeed he did attend to her, as it was; he did his duty conscientiously. He seated himself by her on her arrival and talked to her about her journey. But all the while he felt that the Count and Countess had lent their Viennese eyes to him; and these eyes persisted in seeing in her not a pleasant acquaintance, merely the *bourgeois's* wife, who was beyond the pale of intimacy. Nor were matters mended when afterward she shyly spoke to him about London, and he found that her ideas were confined to Hampstead and Bayswater. He knew when, that same evening, he reflected on how he had behaved to her—he knew that externally he had shown her no want of politeness: but to talk to her had been an effort, and he despised himself for the feeling that made it so. And yet the feeling perversely refused to vanish; and indeed next morning it inclined rather to confirm itself. He took a walk in the park with the Count and Countess. They tried to give him every information he asked for; they renewed their offers of various useful introductions—especially one to Count T——, a great territorial noble, who lived in the neighborhood of the castles he was about to visit; and noticing their charm of manner, their kindness, and their perfect taste, and realizing how their pride was like a dagger which they kept in a velvet sheath, and could never draw, unless someone ventured to attack them, he said to himself that a pride which he shared with them could not after all be so very absurd or vulgar.

In the afternoon they departed. The Princess, when she had seen the last of them, asked Grenville to join with her in her relief at being rid of the lady: and calling the children and her niece to her, began to laugh and talk with them, as if a weight had been lifted from her mind suddenly. He, however, was conscious of a certain blankness. He had a feeling as if his natural allies had deserted him, and had left him in a position more or less false among strangers. But his spirits revived when the Princess, with great good humor, returned after dinner to the subject of his promised expeditions, and arranged that he should start as soon as he felt inclined. "Irma," she said, "goes in a day or two. She is waiting to hear from her doctor about a little watering place between this and Buda-Pesth, to which she wishes to take her children. They are both delicate: neither London nor this place suits them. Had your ways only lain in the same direction you might have waited and taken charge of her."

He was by no means sorry to hear that this was impossible. He had lost his sense of happy ease in the castle, and he felt that a little wandering all by himself would sober him. He hated to feel himself an unsympathizing critic of his hostess, and a supercilious critic of her niece, who was prettier than he first had thought she was. Her eyes would have pleased Greuze; her dress would have pleased Worth; her complexion would have pleased anybody. But he could not help measuring her by the standard given him by the Countess; the chief impression she conveyed to him was that she was not *grande dame;* and the signs of refinement and thought in her by which he was sometimes struck, merely surprised, and did nothing toward attracting him.

The very next morning, for instance, when he was turning over some books in the library, she happened to enter without at first seeing him; and with obvious curiosity began to inspect the shelves. Grenville's only thought was, "What on earth can she want here?" The moment she saw him she started and blushed crimson.

"I'm so sorry," she said. "I didn't mean to disturb you."

She certainly did disturb him; but, seeing that she turned to go, the whole of his good nature was up in arms to reassure her.

"Can I," he said kindly, "help you to look for anything? There's nothing here, I'm afraid, that's very new or amusing."

"I like old books," she faltered, "though I daresay I don't understand them. What I wanted to look at was the castles you showed the Princess."

Grenville produced the volume, and turned over the leaves with her. She seemed unnecessarily grateful for his politeness, and was profuse in her exclamations of interest. The exclamations annoyed him, and he asked her, by way of checking them, if connected as she was with the country, she had seen any of these places herself.

"No," she said. "My mother was Hungarian; but this house and Vienna are nearly all I know of Europe. I have never seen anything. Please don't let me disturb you."

This annoyed him also—this constant tone of apology. He remained with her dutifully till they had come to the last picture; and then with a feeling of relief he escaped to his own bedroom.

"What a difference," he reflected, "between a woman like that and the Countess. The Countess is fifty if she is a day; and never at her best could have been as pretty as Mrs. Schilizzi. But how much more important in mere point of attraction is a certain kind of bearing than beauty of face or form! The Countess has the power of beauty; the other has merely the face of it. The Countess and women like her—their great quality is this: it is self-confidence without self-consciousness, not perhaps with regard to individuals, but with regard to life. This has nothing to do with what we should call knowledge of the world on their part. A girl may have it, just as much as a woman. It is a confidence not in what she has seen, but is the point of view she has seen it from. Take, for instance, Lady Evelyn Standish. She is as innocent of any doubt as to her own point of view, as she is innocent of any knowledge of evil. Between a woman like this and a woman not like this, there is the same difference in the way they deal with life that there is between the touch of different players on the piano.

As he was piecing these thoughts together, he looked out on the park, and there he saw the woman whom he had thus been obliquely criticising. She was with her children under the flickering boughs of the horsechestnut trees. Her dress was creamy brown, with a hat trimmed to match it; theirs was red, making them look like anemones. She was dancing to amuse them with some graceful subdued movement. The sunlight fell on them through the young, expanding leaves; and the group of figures arrested him by its mere charm as a picture. Then its meaning came to his heart and touched him. Feeling seemed to be glancing there under the green shadow. "That," he said to himself, as he stood watching it, "that, I admit, is a perfect piece of nature. Could this woman be as natural with the world as she is with her children, no doubt I should think her charming. Even as it is," he continued mentally, "she is quite pretty enough to suggest one satisfactory thought to me: and that is the thought of how completely the time is past when a woman's prettiness could ever really disturb me."

Turning from the window he took out of a small writing-case the photograph of a girl, with a well-poised head, and eyes that looked with a sort of composed eagerness. "You, dear Evelyn," he murmured, "if ever your love is mine, will never disturb *me:* and I—God help me—will never disturb *you.*"

That evening he wrote in his diary as follows: "My expedition has been definitely arranged. I start the day after to-morrow. The change has come just when it was most wanted. The grievances of the Princess against Viennese society, and the talk and the smart dresses of the young grass-widow from Hampstead, whose husband, it seems, is at Symrna, making a railway, were beginning to interfere with the charm which this place had for me—to interfere with it before I had realized half of it.

"My pride, I suppose, ought to have been flattered by Mrs. Schilizzi, who did me the honor to say that she had read and admired my poems. I did my best to look all that the occasion demanded; and I was in such good humor at the prospect of going to-morrow, that I have no doubt I succeeded. In that prospect I have only one thing to complain of. Count T——, to whom an introduction was offered me, and with whom I might have stayed, is away. I shall, therefore, have to go to an inn, in a village or small town called Lichtenbourg. There is a mineral spring in the place, frequented by a few invalids: so the inn, which my servant knows, and which calls itself the Hotel Imperiale, will no doubt be something more than a mere tavern. But I know these obscure hotels, and at best it will be most uncomfortable. The nearest railway station, too, is nine miles away, and we will have to jolt there in some battered vehicle of the country."

CHAPTER VI.

So far as the railway was concerned, the journey was not formidable. The station at which he was to alight was but forty miles away; and the train being an Hungarian express, took but three hours in reaching it. The weather was now as warm as an English midsummer. Flowers dotted the plains like sparks dropped from a rocket, and there was a sigh, a stir, and a life in the sunlit air as if the lips of the present were expecting those of the future. The groups of peasants and farmers at the intermediate stations seemed to Grenville like happy scenes out of an opera; and some of the simple vehicles which he saw waiting outside did not augur ill for his coming nine miles drive. At his own station, however, a great surprise awaited him. Besides himself there alighted a distinguished looking lady and gentleman, with a couple of footmen, a maid, a pile of dressing-bags, and a poodle; and when Fritz escorted him out through the small booking office, instead of having to look for some varnished cart on springs, he saw before him not only two smart omnibuses, with the name of Lichtenbourg blazoned in gold letters on them, but a collection of landaus far better appointed than most that are to be had on hire at places like Nice or Brighton. A moment later his servant had engaged one of them, and he was presently driving off with a rapid but easy motion. These little touches of modern fashionable civilization gave to his dreamy mood a flavor of mundane piquancy, increasing by contrast the charm of the country he now was entering. It was totally different from that which surrounded the castle of the Princess. First came a mile or so of rich emerald meadows, dotted with quiet cattle; and an old quadrangular manor house, with a tower at each corner, was standing and drowsing knee-deep in the grass. Grenville saw over a hedge its quaint gardens and greenhouses. Then came a line of hills covered with pine and beech; and the road was presently deep in a sylvan valley. The scenery grew by turns wilder and still more smiling. Wooded gorges alternated with pasture and peeping villages and village greens, each of which had its crucifix, with *prie-dieus* and seats before it, for open air devotion. Crucifixes also were curiously frequent along the roads; and nailed to trees from which they could watch the travelers, pictures of saints looked through the leaves like birds. By and by came a region of blooming orchards; then a gorge with a torrent brawling at the bottom; and up in the sky, rising above the foliage, a high roofed castle, whose tower had a copper dome like a soap bubble. "That is Count T——'s," said Fritz, from his seat by the coachman; and Grenville knew he was nearing his destination. He passed a water mill; then came a cottage with an arbor; and on the cottage was painted the words "Wilhelms-Quelle." Similar cottages with the names of other springs on them, succeeded each other at intervals of about a furlong; and judging of his future from the aspect of these primitive establishments, he began to augur for himself but scant luxury for the night. Presently, however, on the side of a swelling hill, he saw extended the line of a long white building, on which, as he approached it, were legible the words "Hotel de Milan." He saw as he passed it a great glazed restaurant, with waiters, and white tables; and beyond was a garden with pavilions in it. "Our hotel *excellenz*," said Fritz, turning round to him, "is in the town. It is much better than this one. The house, the villa in front of us, is the villa of the King of Moldavia."

"Good Heavens," thought Grenville, I never expected this!" On either side of him now were alleys of horsechestnuts, clipped as carefully as a box-hedge in a garden. The road, or the street, as one might call it, dipped over the brow of the hill, and a colony of other villas, with verandas and gay shutters, on various acclivities, were gleaming among clouds of leafage. Presently there came a row of diminutive shops; and opposite them, before the portico of a large building, the carriage drew up. This was the Hotel Imperiale. There was little life stirring; but the establishment was as well appointed as if it had been at Baden-Baden, in the old days of the gambling. It was now nearly seven o'clock; and while Grenville was washing and brushing himself, Fritz ordered dinner for him, and came to guide him to the restaurant. Here was a fresh surprise. The restaurant adjoined the hotel, but was not part of it. It formed one side of a garden, of which the hotel formed another; and the tables were arranged some in a long saloon, some in a veranda, which had the garden under it. In the middle of the garden was a kiosk ready for a band, and on the two other sides of the square were ball rooms, reading rooms, and a theater. The whole place had an air of Baden-Baden in miniature.

But it was a Baden-Baden that was for the present sleeping. The important Frenchman who superintended the restaurant informed Grenville that the season was only just begun—indeed that that day was reckoned the first day of it: and he handed his excellency the opening number of the Visitors' List—a little flimsy sheet with not more than fifty names in it. Lamps were sparkling in the kiosk; dainty tables were laid; Grenville's dinner was really of the most delicate kind: but besides his own, only two tables were occupied; in the garden below was only a loitering group or two; and such voices and the movement of such feet as there were, were oddly audible in the prevalent dreamlike silence.

After dinner he rambled through the little town, with its hilly roadways and masses of mysterious foliage. The fantastic villas gleamed. There was gilding on the gates of some of them. The whole place was kept in faultless neatness. And yet there was no gas; but the clipt horsechestnut alleys were lit with lamps that shone like midsummer glow worms. There were seats in green recesses and wandering paths among verdure. Everything—even the very gravel raked so carefully—teemed with suggestions of unknown fastidious life. Hardly a soul was stirring. It was a silence that seemed to be waiting for the life that would soon come to it—for the floating sounds of bands, for whispers, for women's dresses. It seemed to be waiting for life, like a woman waiting for love. It seemed to be saying, "Here is my heart, fill it."

This subtle impression stole into Grenville's mind, and when he woke next morning it was there like a bunch of violets. He was to start early on one of his expeditions;

and by half-past eight Fritz had a carriage ready for him. Away he drove into the fresh youth of the day, past opened venetian shutters, and bedding hung over window sills. His road for some way was that he had traversed yesterday. The apple blossoms and the gorges again met his eyes. But in his heart and his nerves there was now a new restlessness. All life seemed to be imploring for something, and his own life added its own vague petition. Memories of bygone love affairs, and the longings they had failed to satisfy, began to come down to him in the resinous breaths of the forest, where the dew was still on the leaves of the wild strawberries. He seemed to see the colors of women's dresses, and the flash of women's eyes to whom he could give no name. Even a peasant kneeling at the shrine of a wayside saint quickened in him some sense of vague imaginative expectancy.

It was a day of dreams. The castle—the object of his expedition—was something beyond his wildest hopes. Like the one he had seen already, it covered an isolated rock; only large as that one was, this was three times its size, and was almost ghastly in the completeness of its preservation, like a corpse that is undecayed. The gate tower, the guardroom, the batteries, the long battlemented walls, the fields and orchards inclosed in their vast cincture, the quaint pavilions looking like miniature forts, and lastly the dwelling itself, hugging the edge of a precipice, and reached by three drawbridges—a pile with a hundred windows, crooked arcaded courts, rooms stacked with armor, a suite of Italian halls, and a fossil flower garden with a fountain, that masked the magazines for powder—all this, though deserted excepting by one custodian, had hardly a stone or tile on a roof missing. This overpowering shell of the past, with its strange enchanted silence, seemed to Grenville to be waiting for what had gone, just as Lichtenbourg with its lamps seemed to be waiting for what was coming.

The last of these two impressions became even more vivid that evening. He found when he dined that there were several parties in the restaurant; and afterward the band in the kiosk gave its first performance for the season. There were some listeners under the trees; and a faint whisper of feet; and now and then through the shadow moved the gleam of some rustling toilette. Early next morning he found his way to the springs—very different from the antiquated cottages by the road. They were near together, all of them in a winding garden, which filled with its walks and grass the bottom of a wooded valley. Again the band was playing: some visitors were drinking the waters, the lady and the poodle among them, whom he had seen at the railway station. Some gay parasols made bright patches of color; and here and there, brilliant from banks of leafage, there shone forth masses of blossoming lilac. Grenville wandered about, scanning the people curiously. He was interested to notice in certain of them an air of suppressed fashion; and although presumably they had come most of them for their health, yet they and the scene together were somehow suggestive of dissipation. He had intended that day to have gone on his second expedition; but the life about him stirred his fancy so pleasantly that he determined instead to remain quiet and observe it.

But in an hour or so the gardens were empty, and the

whole town looked deserted: and though a craving for the present, which was mixing itself with his dreams of the past, kept him the whole morning in a state of anxious excitement, a blank reaction came with the afternoon. The silence and the solitude gradually lay like a weight on him. He regretted that he had not got his expedition over; and he longed to be back with the Princess, hearing her pleasant voice again.

Nor were matters mended when he learnt, the last thing at night, that this waste of a day had necessitated the waste of another. The castle he was to see was inhabited: to-morrow it would be closed to visitors, so he would have to wait on, and go there the day after. The intervening time seemed to stretch before him like a desert; and he sank to sleep in a mood of impatient wonder as to how he should get through it. For an hour next morning the scene at the wells amused him. Then again came dullness. In desperation he started on a walk into the country. The scenery was beautiful, but he was not in a mood to enjoy it. On his return to his hotel he thought half the day had been disposed of; but he found, on consulting his watch, that it was only half-past eleven. The gardens were empty, except for two nursery maids. The theater looked as if it would never again be open. The reading room and the conversation room were closed and the blinds down. In the hotel it was evident that one or two rooms were occupied; but the windows of all the rest were sealed hermetically. The town was asleep; hardly a villa was tenanted. He began to loathe the sight of everything—of the tables under the trees, where no one drank coffee, of the green seats on which no one sat, and the paths where no one wandered. He walked so incessantly that at last he became footsore; and everything which but two days ago was so strange and suggestive began to oppress him with a sort of hateful familiarity.

At last his prospects brightened. The dinner hour drew near. He was not hungry; but to eat would at all events be an occupation. In a somewhat happier mood he was strolling in front of the restaurant, looking occasionally at the waiters as they bustled and arranged the tables. The warm daylight was dying in a dim flush, and here and there within doors lamps were being lighted. Nothing was wanting to the scene but the life that it seemed to call for. Suddenly, on turning round he saw moving among the trees the graceful figure of a woman, which at once startled him into interest. Her pale pink dress and black hat, with feathers in it, spoke of the daintiest fashion of Mayfair or of Paris; and there was something in her air and movements, though he could only see her back, which filled him at once with a pleasant sense of curiosity. He took a turn round the kiosk, so as to meet her and see her face. The maneuver was successful. He encountered her. He started—it was Mrs. Schilizzi!

"Good Heavens!" he exclaimed; "and who would have thought to see you here!" He smiled as he spoke, and his manner was more cordial and friendly than it ever had been while they were staying together at the castle. She, on the contrary, looked at him a little coldly, and remained at a distance from him, as if wishing to move on.

"I'm so sorry we troubled you," she said. "It was my aunt who insisted on it. Myself I knew quite well that you were too busy to attend to such matters."

"What on earth do you mean?" exclaimed Grenville, with an accent of bewilderment, which the most suspicious of listeners could not have doubted was genuine. Mrs. Schilizzi did not doubt it, certainly. The slight cloud on her face melted with a naïve quickness. "Tell me!" she exclaimed with a smile. "Didn't you get our telegram?"

"Never," he said. "What telegram?"

"Why," she replied, "just after you left, I heard from my doctor about the place I thought of going to. He said there was scarlatina there; so that put it out of the question; and he strongly recommended that I should bring my children here. My aunt telegraphed at once to you, in my name, begging you to engage some rooms for us; but getting no answer, I came over myself. I thought, too, that before deciding, I might as well see for myself how I liked the looks of things."

At this moment Fritz appeared from the hotel, and as soon as he caught sight of Grenville, hurried up to him with an envelope.

"I shouldn't wonder," said Grenville, "if this were your telegram at last. It is! Well, the mystery explains itself. My name was written *Glanvil*, and the address was 'Hotel de Milan.'"

"Ah," said Mrs. Schilizzi, "that was the agent's fault. He put the address. He thought he knew all about it. This, I find, is the right hotel. I shall settle about our rooms to-morrow; go back in the afternoon, and at once make my arrangements."

"It's a pity," said Grenville civilly, "that you can't

wait a day. In that case we might have gone back together. I propose to-morrow to see one of those old castles."

"How interesting!" she exclaimed, with such an air of sincerity that Grenville doubted for a moment whether he would not ask her to come with him. The idea, however, was interrupted by Fritz, who announced that his dinner was ready; and as Mrs. Schilizzi had ordered hers in her sitting-room, he took himself off, expressing a hope at parting that he might meet her an hour or so later, when the band began its performance. She nodded a pleased assent, and by and by, in the lamplight, he returned to the same spot, and waited for her under the leafy shadows.

"Upon my word, we have smartness here with a vengeance!" he said to himself presently, as a figure in a long pale cloak, that was braided with gold and trimmed with swan's down, came down the steps of the hotel, accompanied by a maid, who was peering about her inquiringly. He at once advanced, and with a smile of happy relief, Mrs. Schilizzi said, "I shouldn't have known where to look for you. One man in the dusk is so much like another."

"You," said Grenville, "at all events, can't say that about women."

She glanced at him timidly, as they seated themselves in view of the kiosk. "Do you mean," she asked, "that my cloak is too smart for this place?"

"Not at all," said Grenville. As he said it he was hardly sincere; but a moment later he felt that he had become so, when he glanced at her face above the swan's down that seemed like a little flower—a flower childishly conscious of the prettiness of its own petals. It was not a face that excited in him any great interest, but the element of childishness which he now began to discover in her, had, in spite of its freshness, a certain something of pathos, and made him feel kindly toward her, as he might have done toward a child. He began to describe to her the wonders of the castle he had visited. She listened intently, taking in every word, and he finally did the thing he had already contemplated. He invited her to come with him to the other castle to-morrow.

"Could I?" she exclaimed. "I wonder if I could manage to wait?" The pleasure of the prospect for her was doubled by the complete surprise. She played with her doubts for a few moments, and then assented, with a soft laugh of delight.

When they parted, which they did before very long, he took another solitary stroll in the lamp-lit horsechestnut alleys; and in a mood of lazy conjecture he began to think her over. One of the things she had said considerably raised his opinion of her. He had happened casually to allude to Countess C——; and Mrs. Schilizzi, with a decision and a discriminaion that struck him, had remarked on the charm of her appearance, and the still greater charm of her manner; adding, "Not that she cares to be nice to me; but she's so self-possessed and natural, there's an artistic pleasure in watching her." "Your aunt's artistic sense," he had answered, "is not quite so developed." Into Mrs. Schilizzi's face had come an expression of humor, as if a piece of gravel had rippled a quiet pool: and she had said, "My aunt thinks that the Countess snubs her." The words were commonplace enough; but her tone and expression in saying them seemed to Grenville as he called her image back to him, to show the keenest and yet the gentlest sense of the whole facts in question. And yet that this should be so was a puzzle, rather than a pleasure, to him. He tried to figure to himself Mrs. Schilizzi in London; and the only place at home into which he could possbily fit her was not one that seemed consistent with much social discrimination. He thought of the pretty faces, and the dresses just as pretty, that on any June morning might be seen thronging the Row. He thought of how many of those faces had no name or meaning, in the only world which he or his friends knew. And then he thought of others, whose names were perhaps known to him, and who at least suggested a definite social type. But it was a type that to him was more distasteful than any. It was that of the women who are fashionable in everything except in fact—the adored of youthfnl guardsmen—the heroines of the river and of Hurlingham: and in his own mind he classed Mrs. Schilizzi as one of these. He pictured her drawing-room, with men much at their ease in it, lounging on divans and sofas, and playing impertinently with her knick-knacks, while she lounged also, resenting nothing that was said to her. This did not make him forgetful of what he thought were her merits; nor did it, indeed, make him think of her less good-naturedly: but it did prevent him feeling the pleasure he might have felt in the prospect of having tomorrow so pretty an appreciative a companion.

CHAPTER VII.

By a quarter of ten the following morning a smart looking victoria stood at the hotel door; and Grenville was smoking a cigarette with the air of a man waiting. The carriage, in fact, had been there for something like twenty minutes, and his face had begun to wear a slight shade of annoyance, though it was the annoyance of resignation rather than that of impatience. At last a voice was heard within on the staircase—the voice of a lady calling out to her maid. "Julie," it was saying, "this is really too bad of you. You first give me my wrong dress, and now these gloves are both for my left hand. Take them away, and bring me some others instantly." There was a certain note of temper in all this which, for the moment, slightly jarred upon Grenville. The impression, however, was instantly done away with, when the same voice was heard, with completely restored good-humor and also with a softness in it, full of a quick repentance, saying "Oh, Julie, thank you—these are just what I wanted." A pale brown dress, the color of which Grenville recognized, gleamed through the shadow of the hall; and Mrs. Schilizzi issued.

Her lips, and her eyes also, were full of apologies for her lateness; and the flush in her cheeks showed the sincerity of her emotion. "I *am* so sorry," she repeated as soon as they were settled in the carriage. "Waiting is a thing I never could bear myself." She turned her eyes, and the brown feathers of her hat, to him, her chin hiding itself in the sable about her collar—turned them, with an air that might have seemed to be asking for admiration, if it had not, with such naïve frankness, asked for pardon instead. Grenville's pleasant answer disarmed her timidity. "My maid," she went on, "was so stupid. She gave me the wrong dress. I only saw it was the wrong one when it was on: and then I had to change it. This suits me to-day so much better than the other."

"What!" said Grenville; "do your frocks change their colors, like a chameleon?"

"No," she replied. "But I change: and this is the color that suits me best when I am happy." Here she broke into a little musical laugh, which died in her eyes into a look of returning timidity, as she added, "Mr. Grenville, you will think I am very silly?"

Grenville thought she was, but was too civil to say so: and yet at the same time he had some undefined impression that the silliness, such as it was, was a thing on the surface only; and he felt, as they drove off among the villas and the horsechestnuts, a pleasure in the sense of sharing with her the soft air of the morning, and all the day's prospects which it seemed to breathe in their faces. This impression deepened as from time to time he glanced at her, and he saw how fresh was the pleasure that she herself was experiencing. He had thought that her face was like a flower yesterday evening. It was now like a flower with the dew on it, tremulous with life and brightness. At first, however, he was annoyed by the frequency of the exclamations with which she called attention to this thing or that thing—the shining roof of a villa, a hedge, or even a column of smoke: but he gradually realized that, common as these objects were, there was something distinctive in the aspect of each as she noticed it—some effect of light, some tender contrast of color, which, when it was pointed out to him, he at once appreciated, but which, had he been by himself, would have altogether escaped him.

"Oh," she exclaimed at last, drawing a long breath, "look at that! Look! Do let us stop the carriage."

The carriage was stopped; and then, with an amused perplexity, he turned round to her, asking her: "Well, what is it?"

She pointed to an orchard of cherry blossom. He had himself already remarked it—a feature of the landscape, a part of its passing pageant. But to her it had a beauty in itself, peculiar to that moment. "Do you see the petals?" she said. "They palpitate like the wings of butterflies."

There was in her voice an almost religious tone, like that of a child repeating a hymn with feeling. She saw he understood her, and gave him a glance of gratitude; and then her gravity, like a small wave on the sand, sparkled and broke into a laugh of unconscious happiness.

"I," said Grenville, as the carriage moved on again, "enjoy nature in some ways; but I never saw anyone so sensitive to its beauty as you. I have learnt much from you during the last ten minutes. The spring is showing me beauties that never before were visible."

She turned to him, blushing crimson, with an expression of startled pain. "How can you say so?" she faltered. "You are laughing at me. I could not teach anything to anybody—and to you least of all people!"

"Indeed," said Grenville kindly, "you do me a great wrong. I was not laughing. I meant what I said, literally."

"Of course," she went on only partially reassured, "you understand nature—a great poet like you. You can describe it—you can express its meaning. I can only feel it, and I am foolish to show my feelings. But a minute ago I was so happy that I forgot myself."

"It is you," said Grenville, "who are laughing at me now. Me a great poet! I published one small volume, which only my friends read: and they have now forgotten it. It was a piece of myself, perhaps; but it was not a piece of literature."

"Yes," she said, "that was its great charm. Most books are books. Your book was a person. I was not one of your friends; but I read it, and have never forgotten it. I bought a copy; and mother told me I was so extravagant. All you said about nature—it moved me even more than Keats does. What you said about other things I didn't understand then."

Grenville now began to notice in her one characteristic which interested him. Her mood seemed to change like an English sky in April. At one moment she would be hidden behind some cloud of shyness; the next she would brighten, and show, with a happy unconscious confidence, herself and her slightest thoughts as the sky shows its blueness.

"I'll tell you," he said, "what I think about your appreciation of nature. You realize how beautiful it is in itself. What I attend to most is, the human thoughts it stirs in me. Look about you at the valley we now are entering. Look at these wayside crosses! And there—nailed against that pine tree, do you see the picture of St. Joseph—so uncouth and so simple? And those peasants, too, in the wood, tugging at their unfortunate cart horse—to me they seem the serfs of some phantom baron. The whole place is full of the air of the Middle Ages, and all my imagination is troubled by the smell of the pine trees."

She looked about her, taking in every detail, a new excitement changing her whole expression. "Ah!" she exclaimed, "you are right. This is just like a fairy tale. See that little gray building; it must, I am sure, be a hermitage. And where does the baron live? And do you think there are robbers? Nothing seems real except you, and the carriage, and my frock. Do go on; I want you to tell me more."

"Well," he replied, entering readily into her mood, "the farther we drive the deeper we are getting into fairyland, and the place we shall reach at last is a genuine fairy castle. It is not a ruin; it is lived in; it is full of all sorts of splendors, that are hidden away under its moss-grown roofs and pinnacles. It belongs to a mysterious Count, who spent all his youth in the East, and returned to Europe laden with gold and jewels. As to this I am serious: I am not romancing. The people at the hotel told me his whole history. He is a Polish count, and also an Egyptian Pasha. The castle is very old. There is a picture of it in the book I showed you; but what it is like now I know no better than you."

She leaned back silently, smiling at her own thoughts: then suddenly she looked up at him, and said, laughing into his eyes, "And tell me—do tell me—will there be ghosts, and drawbridges—and a chapel, and dungeons, and winding stairs and balconies? You, who have seen so much, can hardly tell how excited I am!"

She was so completely natural, and there was in her spirits something not only so buoyant but, at the same time, so confiding, that Grenville was charmed by it into a curious sense of intimacy with her. He felt that they were playfellows sharing the same holidays.

"Do," she went on presently, "do promise me that there will be balconies, with rusty iron scrollwork, beautifully wrought. I am sure there will be; and from one of them a princess used to look into the distance, waiting perhaps for something that never came." The laugh had died out of her voice, as she uttered these last words. They fell from her lips with a slow, meditative softness. "Do you," she said, "understand how my thoughts wander?"

"Yes," he answered, "and mine are wandering with them."

For a time they hardly spoke. They had left the more beaten road, and were ascending a rugged track, which climbed up a wooded hillside, and from which nothing but wood was visible. The smells of bark and of eaves became pungent about them. Some wild-eyed charcoal burners scrambled down a bank, with baskets on their bowed backs, and stared after the carriage. Presently came the cottage of a forester, with some wolves' heads nailed against it. These Grenville pointed out to his companion, who laid her hand on his arm, with an impulse of imaginative terror.

"Well," he said to her, "and what do you think now?

Does not the mystery of the forest seem to be closing round us?"

For an hour the journey continued to be of this character.

At last, however, after a number of ups and downs, they emerged on some sloping grass land, with a timbered farmhouse belonging to it, which bore the date of 1490, and on one of whose gable ends was a quaint Madonna fading. A little farther on came hedges that showed signs of clipping. A shed stood by the road, with some carts and plows under its shelter; and a moment later, without any warning, the carriage had stopped before the gateway of a discolored turreted pile, the extent and the situation of which was made doubtful by the trees surrounding it. A porter unbarred the doors, and bowing obsequiously to the visitors, admitted them to a court, narrow, but of great length, entirely surrounded by buildings, and having flower beds and lilac bushes in the middle. Their career of sightseeing was apparently all marked out for them. They were taken up a flight of fantastic steps, which brought them to an open arcade, running all the length of the court; and down this they were led to a cluster of towers at the end of it. A series of loopholes pierced in the outer wall showed them as they passed that the castle was on the shoulder of a hill, and gardens and tree tops were visible far below them. A small door opened, and they were treading on an Italian pavement: they were startled by a glitter of profuse and barbarous gilding, by purple portieres, and fanciful Moorish looking-glasses. These decorations belonged to a sort of vestibule; and out of this, by various crooked passages, and through more portieres, they passed to a nest of bedrooms. The situation of all of them was romantic and picturesque in the extreme. They occupied strange towers and angles of the ancient building, and looked down over the green depths below: but their furniture and their decorations were of the strangest kind imaginable. The beds, fantastic in shape, were draped in cloth of gold, the dressing-tables were garnished with pictures of Oriental dancing girls, the ormolu frames of which glittered with enamel and turquoise; silver stars and crescents studded the ceilings, and crimson rugs glowed on the polished floors. Presently they found themselves in the Count's private apartments. His bed had legs of ivory. The quilt was almost covered by an embroidered coronet; a painted coronet covered the bottom of his bath; above his washhand stand were twenty bottles of essences, and his jug and basin—both enormous—were of silver. Then, by means of many tortuous staircases, they reached what originally had been the banqueting hall of the castle. It was long and low, with a roof of ponderous vaulting, but the Count had seen fit to relieve this with florid gilding. There was a Mosaic pavement, as slippery and as shining as ice, and the furniture looked like the stock of a bric-a-brac dealer in Florence. From this they passed into a long suite of rooms—a billiard-room, hung with jeweled Oriental weapons, a drawing-room, where everything—even the legs of the tables—was ultramarine, a grand saloon surrounded by Gobelin tapestry, a dining-room, an antechamber, and last of all a chapel, where the walls were dim with monumental tablets and kneeling knights carved in discolored marble, and where a golden lamp in the silence was burning before the altar.

This apparently ended the general routine of sight-seeing, but Fritz, industrious as ever on behalf of his master's dignity, had meanwhile been impressing the greatness of it on a fat, supercilious looking seneschal; and the visitors were accordingly informed that if they would like to use it for their luncheon there was a room with a fine view, which would be very much at their service. The offer was accepted. The room was in one of the towers, and, owing to some lucky circumstance, it had escaped scot-free from the irrepressible taste of the Count. The walls were whitewashed, the floor bare; the cabinets, chairs, and tables were of dark worm-eaten walnut; and in a corner was an old spinet.

"Here," exclaimed Grenville, "is the castle in its natural state. The ghosts of the past, I am sure, must make this their refuge." He went to the window, which he opened. "Mrs. Schilizzi," he said, "come here, let me beg of you, and see your dream realized." She went toward him, and they stepped out on a balcony—a balcony whose railings were of beautiful old wrought iron. To right and left of them were irregular bulging towers, and steeped tiled roofs spiked with fantastic ornaments. Below them a wood of beech trees descended the precipitous hillside, and from the bottom of this an expanse of country spread itself, reaching away to hills on the far horizon. Mrs. Schilizzi said nothing, but leaned on the rusty iron, and seemed lost in the prospect. He watched her dainty figure against the background of weather-beaten wall. Her look and attitude were grave and more absorbed than he had ever seen them hitherto, and though her expression was not what would be necessarily called religious, she made him think of St. Monica and the balcony of the house at Ostia. "I suppose," he said at last, "you are fulfilling your own scripture. You seem to be waiting for the something that never comes."

She turned her eyes to him. They seemed to be full of dreams, as a pool when it ceases to sparkle becomes full of reflections. Then, as if to perplex him, the sparkle came suddenly back again, and she said, "Do you mean that I seem to be waiting for our luncheon?"

"For that," said Grenville, "you need, at any rate, wait no longer. See! our table is spread. Was anything ever so charming?"

Mrs. Schilizzi, as she moved to take her seat, opened the old spinet, and struck a jangling chord on the keys. "There!" she exclaimed, "now I have done with dreaming. Mr. Grenville, all this is making me quite beside myself. Perhaps I shall be better after I have eaten something."

One of the servants brought in a bowl of lilacs, which he placed on the table, by way of a simple ornament. She gave an exclamation of pleasure at sight of the delicate color. "A thing like that," she said, "always puts me in spirits."

As they eat their cold provisions they began to talk over the castle, and Grenville enlarged on the extreme interest of it as a building, and the grotesque misfortune that had befallen it through the taste of its present owner.

"You shouldn't," she said, "talk about that. You are spoiling everything. I suppose it's vulgar, if you come to take it to pieces; but here in this forest, I think one's imagination alters it; and it's splendid for the time, if one only believes it's splendid."

"Yes," said Grenville, "I think you are right there. Ridiculous and vulgar as all these splendors are, they are, at the same time, so audacious, so barbarous, and so insolent, that they load one's mind with some odd sense of romance. A place like this would in England be quite impossible."

"I feel," she said, "that I hardly know where I am— where, or in what century. I don't believe that I ever thought much about such things before; but what you used to say to my aunt—you didn't say much to me— somehow seemed to open a new door in my mind."

Grenville was again conscious of an anxiety to avoid conversation that was personal: so he said, "But surely, so far as regards the *where*, you must know this country as well as you know England."

"You underestimate," she said, "my capacity for knowing little. Haven't I, Mr. Grenville, told you so much already? My aunt's castle—I know the four walls of that. I know my husband's flat in Vienna, the Prater, and the opera house. I know nothing besides, but Countess D——'s villa in Hungary."

"Who," asked Grenville, "is Countess D——?"

"My cousin," she said. "Mother was a Hungarian. She was very poor, but of very good family—you must not think me boastful for saying that; only except Alma D—— her relations are all dead: and Alma's villa was new and might have been anywhere; and outside its grounds all that I saw was fields. As to Vienna," she went on after a pause, "of course a person like myself— the wife of a Greek engineer—is nobody and sees nothing. I am there either a prisoner or a tourist. Considering that, till I married, I lived always with ladies and gentlemen, it is a little odd sometimes to feel myself in that position—not" she added, "that in London, or, rather, at Hampstead, I am anybody. I am very provincial at the best of times; or, perhaps, if I had only the courage, I ought to call myself by the terrible word suburban."

Grenville for various reasons was struck and interested by her manner. There was in it not only a certain plaintive prettiness, but a humor and dignity, when she passed these criticisms on herself, which was, in his judgment, quite enough to refute them.

"I never," he said, "saw anyone who was less provincial than you."

"Well," she replied, "I won't argue the point. If you ever see more of me I shall have little need to do so."

When their luncheon was over, and they were once more in the carriage, with a naïve abruptness she recurred to the same subject. As they drove away she turned to look at the castle, and said, with a slight sigh, "Perhaps one reason why I feel so *borné* is not that I have seen so few things, but that I long to see many. And yet, after all, inexperience has its advantages. A person who had not seen so little as I have, I am sure could have never enjoyed a day so much."

"You cannot," said Grenville, "have enjoyed it more than I have: though I have enjoyed it for a reason that could never be shared by you."

"What reason?" she asked.

"The reason is," he replied, "that I have had you as a companion."

The moment he had said the words he repented of them. The compliment was obvious, and had slipped from him, out of some forgotten habit; but the effect it had upon her touched his heart like a knife. She gave him first a look of surprise and pleasure, which shamed him by its trust in his sincerity; then came what seemed reaction of doubt, and a pained resentment. The jolting of the carriage for a time made further speaking impossible. She had turned away from him; but for many minutes afterward he saw, as often as he glanced at her, that a deep flush in her cheek kept coming and going as if her heart were in some hidden tumult. A sudden sense came over him of the nature of the life beside him—of how delicate it was, how easily pleased and wounded; and he said to himself, with an almost disproportionate compunction, which was, however, wholly without vanity, "idiot that I am—what little care I take of her

" I that would not let e'en the winds of heaven
Visit her face too roughly."

By and by, in a totally changed tone, full of sympathy, but without a suspicion of compliment, he took up the conversation as if nothing had interrupted it. "I can hardly admit," he said, "that the pleasure you have taken in our expedition, and which, as I told you just now, has so added to mine, is due to the mere accident of your not having traveled much. Travel more, as no doubt you will some day; and each new climate you visit will call forth new flowers in your mind. Different countries to me are like different muscial instruments, touching into vitality different sets of sympathies, and giving to life the allurement of a different face. I wonder if you will catch my meaning. The Scottish

Highlands, purple with autumn air—the mountains, whose sides are creased with rocky shadows, or which lift themselves through the mist on each other's shoulders into the clouds, the eyes of the moorland children on the bare hillside at evening, all seem to speak to me some one secret of the universe. This land of castles and pine woods, and foresters with plumes and hunting horns, says something wholly different. It makes life speak through a different musical instrument. And the very thought of a Mediterranean sky fills my mind with visions of statued gardens, of ceilings frescoed with all the gods of Olympus, and of purple evenings seen through bowers of Banksia roses. Did you ever," he added, "read the story of Pyramus, who died at the foot of the mulberry tree, and whose blood gave its color to the fruit? All these various civilizations in the same way color the flowers of the mind—ancient Rome or the Renaissance, or the age of chivalry, or the age of the Highland chieftains."

He was not looking at her as he spoke, but he instinctively knew that she was attending to him. He was, therefore, surprised when, at this point, she hastily murmured "Don't," and turned her head away from him.

"Why?" he said, "what is it? Tell me—have I been boring you?"

She looked him in the face, and her eyes were tremulous with tears. "You only," she said, "give me longings for what I shall never know."

When he spoke again, it was in a mere commonplace tone. "You shouldn't," he said, "take so gloomy a view of your future. You should light it up with happier expectations, and with as many of these as possible,

Expectations are like lamps, which it costs nothing to keep burning, and events can only blow out one at a time."

After this, there was an end of seriousness and sentiment, and their talk became nothing but the ripple of meeting sympathies, till once again they saw the villas of Lichtenbourg, and agreed that they would dine in the restaurant, keeping each other company.

Between their return and dinner, she had completed her arrangements about her rooms; and the prettiness of the salon she had secured, and the comfort of the rooms for her children, filled her with spirits and pleasure, as if they were some new toy. She talked about them to Grenville with an innocent and happy volubility which secured his interest by taking his interest for granted, and then from her rooms she passed on to her children, telling him of their lessons, their health, their tastes, their characters—moving from subject to subject lightly and tenderly as a butterfly. Grenville listened, absorbed, wondering why he did so. It was hardly so much words that he was listening to, as a kind of moral music; and when dinner was over he looked back at it with wonder, reflecting that the conversation, which had made it pass so quickly, had hardly strayed beyond the limits of a stranger's nursery.

Again, in the warm evening, they sat under the lamp-lit trees, listening to the cadence of the band. By this time she was silent. Her eyes and her lips were pensive. "Listen," she murmured, as a gay waltz being ended, the music turned into something that might have been a love song or a hymn. Touched by the sound, Grenville said to her softly, "How fond you are of your children.

Whether you see much of the world or little, you at all events have them."

"Yes," she said, and her words kept time to the music, as if she trusted it half to hide and half to express her emotion, "they are all I have to live for."

Presently, as if feeling that she had betrayed more than she meant to, she turned to him with a smile that was at once bright and languid, and thanking him for the pleasure he had that day been the means of giving her, said she was tired, and must now be going to rest. "You have been so kind," she added. "I shall always think of you as one of the kindest people I have known."

"And I," he answered, "I shall always think of you——" He paused.

"Yes," she said, "yes. Tell me how you will think of me?"

She put the question with an undisguised curiosity; but before he had attempted to answer, she had risen, and with her eyes on the ground, said, "If you think of me at all, I will tell you how to do so. Think of me as someone waiting for something that never comes."

CHAPTER VIII.

THE following morning they returned together to the Princess. But everything now was changed, without any apparent reason. Their intimacy of the preceding day, which had blossomed so quickly, had given place to a certain kind of reserve. It was with him that the change originated; but she had been affected by it instantly. When they talked during the journey, it was merely about the most commonplace matters; and for long periods they were both completely silent, she self-wounded by thoughts of what now seemed to her to be folly, and blushing at every stab which she gave to her own nerves; he conscious of a cold mood at work in him, which shut her out from any but his most superficial sympathies.

On reaching the castle, he found a fresh packet of letters. He had not time before dinner to do more than glance at two of them; but the glance, hasty at it was, seemed to confirm him in his present mood; and he muttered as he was brushing his hair, "What an idiot I was yesterday!" The same influence was at work in him during dinner, though it showed itself in a different way. He troubled himself to make conversation; and he made it with some success. He described Lichtenbourg; he described the castles he had visited; he laughed at the Pasha's furniture, at his bath, and at his bottles of essences; and he said to the Princess, "The whole time

I was there, I was in my own mind trying to construct a picture of him. I felt sure he had waxed mustaches, hair dyed and curly, and round his eyes the wrinkles of seventy years' misconduct."

The Princess was delighted, and thought he had never been so pleasant before. As for Mrs. Schilizzi, she looked at him half bewildered, wondering if this could be really her late sympathetic companion. There was nothing in what he said that was really hard or ill-natured; but through it all ran a vein of contemptuous flippancy which made him seem to her quite a different person: and when a little later his tone became more grave, and he discussed with the Princess the characters of certain English statesmen, and mentioned that from two of them he had heard that very evening, she felt him to have retreated farther from her than ever. Till they separated for the night she hardly again addressed him: but then, as she turned to go, a part of what was in her mind expresssed itself.

"I ought," she said, "to thank you again for that delightful expedition of yesterday: but don't"— and her lips as well as her voice trembled—"don't laugh at me for all the nonsense I talked to you. How could I have done so? I can hardly bear to think of it."

"Laugh at you!" he exclaimed. "My dear Mrs. Schilizzi, if your conversation were the kind of thing to be laughed at, I only wish I had friends who would make me laugh oftener."

His voice was full of a genial and hearty frankness which certainly showed her that her request was quite unnecessary; but it wounded her more than it would have done had it been less prompt in its assurance, because it showed so little comprehension of the doubts it dispelled so carelessly. When she reached her room she sank into a chair before the looking-glass, and sat abstractedly staring at her own reflection. At last she was startled at seeing tears gathering in her eyes. She rose abruptly, and hid her face in her pillow. "Never, never, never," she murmured, sobbing, "never again will I show my thoughts to anyone. The moment I do so, something or other nips them, and they lie on my mind like so many withered flowers." The image of Grenville had no part in her trouble, except as a far-off figure which pointed to her own loneliness: and by and by, when she sank into a weary sleep, there was still a line of pain on her upturned childish forehead.

Grenville, meanwhile, was in a very different mood. He was seated at his writing-table, with all the air of a man who has work before him of an anxious and urgent kind: and a certain letter was absorbing his whole attention. It came from his man of business; and its purport was not agreeable. It told him that an old aunt of his, his nearest living relative, who depended for the decencies, if not for the necessaries of her life, on a few hundreds a year which he allowed her out of his limited income, had reduced herself, by a foolish speculation, to temporary but extreme distress. She had incurred liabilities the nature of which she had not properly understood; and for the time being she was left practically penniless. "Unwilling," the writer continued, "to apply for help to you, who have done and who do so much for her, she hoped by selling a little plate, and by practicing various economies, to be able to get through the crisis, without your hearing of its occurrence: but you will see from the details, which I enter on a separate sheet, that this was quite impossible. When I last saw her—she has consulted me several times—I found that she had discharged all but one of her servants; it was a chilly day, and there was hardly any fire in her grate, and I noticed that her hands were trembling, not with agitation only, but with cold. To relieve her effectually, about two hundred and fifty pounds will be required; and reluctant as I am to appeal to you in the matter, under the circumstances I feel I am bound to do so—though I do so without her knowledge. For her immediate wants I have advanced her a small sum myself."

Grenville laid the letter down with a frown of amazed perplexity. "Two hundred and fifty pounds," he said to himself. "I much doubt if I have as much at my banker's." There came to his lips a slight contemptuous smile. "Here am I," he reflected, "thinking myself a great man; flattered by ambassadors, bowed down to by officials, received by hotel keepers as some wonderful *grand seigneur*, and comporting myself as if nothing and nobody were good enough for me: and yet if I write a check for a paltry sum like this, I should be for the time a beggar. I should hardly have money enough to carry me back to England. All the fine fortunes I have fancied myself already possessed of are no more help to me now than the sight of land to a swimmer, who will probably—and this may be my own case—drown before he reaches it. Anyhow let me know the worst."

He turned to his banker's book; and half flinching as he did so, began to examine his account

"It is worse than I thought," he said. "I have barely a hundred left. Up to three hundred, no doubt I could overdraw; but supposing I pay this money, how shall I stand myself?" For the least selfish of men this would have been a very natural question; but even before he had answered it, he considered one point as settled—and that was his payment of the whole sum required. The economies that would be necessary on his own part he now proceeded to calculate; and he soon decided, although with extreme reluctance, that he would have to cut short his travels, and at once return to London.

Quickly as his decision was taken, it was taken with a pang of disappointment, which he bore in the best way possible by refusing to think how keen it was. With a nervous haste he passed to his other letters, as if he counted on finding in them some help to distraction. He began with the two which he had glanced at before dinner: and if he sought distraction, they were unexpectedly successful in bringing it to him. One was from no less a person than the Prime Minister himself; and contained a compliment which he had never expected from that quarter—a request for his opinion on certain important matters, which would form the subject of an impending debate in Parliament. The other was from the Chancellor of the Exchequer, which was even more encouraging. "I cannot," it said, "too highly praise you for the extreme lucidity of your last communication—especially those parts of it in which you work out your suggestions, with regard to the claims of the Turkish and Egyptian bondholders. I believe that with you, and with you alone will be the credit of showing us our way out of an extremely troublesome difficulty. I may tell you that Lord Solway—by the by, is he a relation of yours?—who is an authority of considerable weight on most of our Eastern questions, was asking me about you only two nights ago: and I said to him just what I have said to yourself now. His answer was, 'Then, by G——, he has done more for the Government than if he had won a dozen contested seats.'"

Grenville now turned to an envelope which he had not yet opened, and which in one corner bore the signature "Solway." Its contents were as follows:

"My dear Mr. Grenville: If only your grandfather, whom I remember well, had not been a person of such nice social taste, and had appreciated less keenly the privilege of consorting with the First Gentleman in Europe, you would yourself be in a position to aspire, without arrogance, to the hand of any young lady, no matter how distinguished, provided that her father was not a king or a nobody. But as matters stand, there is hardly a mother in England—I refer to mothers of daughters in any way suitable to yourself—who would not object to you in the character of a son-in-law quite as openly as she would value you in the character of a friend. You are, indeed, an excellent example of the way, so much admired by the pious, in which Providence visits on the children the sins and extravagances of the fathers. As you are not, however, a nonconformist minister, you will, I trust, not be shocked at me when I tell you of my own conviction, that half our duty to Providence consists in dishing it, and, if we cannot get rid of errors, at least getting rid of their consequences. I propose, therefore, if you will allow me, to do this in your own case. I know by this time quite enough of what there is in you to be satisfied that you have before you a brilliant and serviceable career; and I will impute your success to you before you have actually achieved it. Why should you waste any longer time in waiting? If you can manage to do so, you may propose to my niece to-morrow. I don't advise you to do so, for it would have to be done by telegraph; but at all events use whatever expedition you can: and I will tell you how, without the telegraph, you can be quite as expeditious as is necessary. My sister and her two daughters are just starting for Italy. They are going to Milan, Padua, Vicenza, and at last to Venice. I will send you to-morrow an exact calendar of their movements; and then, my advice is, join them. And now, by way of saying something specially pleasant at parting, I may as well tell you this. Evelyn's cousin—young Oliver Jackson—a good-looking boy, but to my mind an insufferable prig, has excited her admiration by the degree he has taken at Oxford, and—people think I'm blind, but I see as much as the best of them—has been lending her books, which she takes and reads with gratitude. There's nothing in this thus far. It's all very silly and natural; but none the less you must remember, as Byron said from experience, 'There is a tide in the affairs of women.' And if you don't know that by this time, I needn't attempt to teach it to you."

As Grenville read this, something that was not trouble exactly, but excitement mixed with anxiety, not only took possession of his face, but also expressed itself in his movements. He rose from his seat, paced the room restlessly, smoked some cigarettes in order to calm his nerves, and finally, with an impatient rapidity, undressed himself and went to bed.

Early next morning he sent a note to the Princess, to tell her he was needed in England, and must start that afternoon for Vienna. She was sincerely annoyed at this, and when she met him at luncheon, she was armed with a piece of news which made her regret stronger. She put into his hand a picture she had just received from the agent—a picture of a castle on the summit of a wooded rock. "Could you only have stayed," she said, "you might easily have seen that. It is said to be by far the most curious place in the country." The moment he looked at it, it struck him as being familiar; and he presently recognized it as the castle which he had seen with such wonder from the railway. He eyed the picture wistfully, and a strong wish came over him not to quit these regions of yet unexhausted dreams. He passed it to Mrs. Schilizzi, who took it with a distant smile. When she examined it, she softly exclaimed, "How curious!" That was her only comment, but she kept it beside her plate, and throughout the meal her eyes were continually turning to it.

As for Grenville, whatever his regrets were, they did not interfere with the decision and promptness of his movements. There was a train for Vienna at five in the afternoon, going by the direct route, and arriving early in the morning: and by it he had arranged to take his departure. The station for this was seven or eight miles distant; so his hours with his friends were already almost numbered. "I suppose," he said to the Princess, "if I am not wanted at home, you will let me come back and finish my explorations?"

"Do," she said, brightening up at the idea. "You must remember I feel you are treating me very badly. However, I'll come to the door with you, and give you a parting kick."

Mrs. Schilizzi came too, with her pair of fair-eyed children, and watched with a quiet face the carriage disappear from the archway.

The mellowed sunshine rendered the drive delightful; and Grenville was in a mood not unfit to enjoy it. But he could not help reflecting for the first mile or so, on another drive he had taken only two days ago, when he had had a companion by his side and had seemed to be drifting into fairyland. But he soon shook off this not very violent sentiment and turned his thoughts on his own situations and prospects. His immediate financial difficulties he viewed with diminished anxiety; and though a journey to Italy would be a new strain on his resources, he felt confident he should manage to meet it somehow. But one thought, which had been forced on him last night, had become more startling and more persistent than ever; and this was the thought of the extreme weakness and insecurity of his own position in the world, as it actually was at present. Another such claim as that which he was now about to meet would reduce him to penury. A fall of five shillings in the rent of each of his acres, would reduce him to ruin yet more complete and hopeless. Nothing but his wits would be left him between himself and starvation. Many people, he reflected, considered him as a social light. He seemed to himself but a small flickering taper, which the slightest breath might at any moment extinguish.

He allowed his mind to dwell upon, and even exaggerate, facts like these, in order to add to the value of the release from them that was being now made so easy for him; and without intentionally constructing any picture of his future, details of it unbidden thrust themselves in upon his consciousness. He saw his name in half the papers of Europe. In various capitals, and at Vienna especially, he saw himself the object of peculiar social consideration. In London his lodgings, and his one man servant, gave place to a large and decorous house and household. He saw a star in his coat, and a phantom ribbon across his breast. From time to time also he saw at his side a wife. Now her happy eyes were making a light in his solitude; now he and she were being announced at some brilliant party. And yet all these images, somehow to his own surprise, pleasing as they were, did but excite him moderately.

"I wonder," he thought, as he found himself alone in the railway carriage, "if from everything in life that we desire, the best part of its charm takes flight as we approach it, or becomes invisible, like a rainbow. I wonder if a political career will prove to be as unrewarding as poetry, as thought, or that life of waking dream, from which even now I find it hard to tear myself. No," he said to himself, "it can hardly be as unrewarding as those. I am only at this moment a little out of conceit with it, because I am annoyed at this sudden disturbance of my arrangements. The best of good things should not be so brusquely thrust on one."

Thus reflecting, he unpacked some refreshments he had taken with him, and trusted that after his meal he should find himself in healthier spirits. He also produced some photographs, which, as he ate his sandwiches, he kept regarding with a grave and meditative attention. One was a portrait of a girl—the same which, a few days since, he had turned to and apostrophized in his bedroom at the Princess's castle; most of the others were views of a park and an old house. The park was evidently beautiful, although even in the photographs a broken bridge and a half-roofless boat house betrayed poverty and neglect. The house too, to the eyes of Grenville, its owner, told the same story. Certain marks on the roof, certain iron ties visible on the walls, meant for him that it was fast falling to pieces, that the present tenants would soon find it uninhabitable; while years of his present income would not suffice to repair it. But his eyes also saw in what indeed would have been seen by anybody—as perfect a specimen as the heart or head could desire of an early Jacobean manor house. There it stood, with its lines of mullioned windows, with its twisted pillars and chimney-stacks, with its domed turrets and its vanes, facing the present with a forlorn, pathetic dignity. But dignity was far from being the only suggestion it conveyed to him. It brought back to him his own early days, and the growing embarrassments of his family. He remembered the straitened life that was masked by those stately walls—the few servants, the wilderness of unused rooms, the meager fare, the one horse in the stables. He remembered his discovering and his boyish inability to believe it that his people used in the country to be talked of as "Those poor Grenvilles." He remembered how the wife of a stockbroker who had intrigued herself into London society and had taken a place in the neighborhood with some of the best shooting in England, had brought to a country ball an omnibus load of lords and ladies, and on the strength of her diamonds and her company had presumed to be condescending to his mother. Memory after memory of the same kind came back to him, each with the sting in it of some humiliating circumstance. Then from the views of his own house, he turned to one of another. This was a plain structure, with a center and two wings, all whitewash and windows, except for an entrance portico. It was bald and hideous, and of no exceptional size; but even the photograph showed that it was kept in perfect order; and its hideousness, as every detail of it proclamied, was at least made respectable by having lasted a hundred years. "And so," thought Grenville, "that is to be my wife's dowry, given her with the special purpose of saving her husband's fortunes, and calling life back to those old walls that are dying. It will be quite sufficient, if only we take our time; and I can solace my pride with this reflection certainly—that if the two properties are united, I shall not only have saved my own, but have given to my wife something that is worth saving."

He replaced the pictures in the case from which he had taken them; and leaning back, he began, with a gathering frown, to see certain facts facing him which were not quite satisfactory. These had reference to his position with regard to the lady whom he had, in his thoughts about the future, been so confidently regarding as his wife. He felt that now, suddenly and for the first time, he realized all that depended on her actually and immediately becoming so; and an event which he had assumed as certain, when looked on as indefinitely distant, began to seem painfully doubtful when abruptly brought so close to him. He set himself to consider what grounds he had for his confidence. They were not so slight as might be perhaps supposed. A man's experience of women may be of two kinds, of which, in proportion as they each become more extensive, the one blunts the perceptions, while the other makes them more delicate. Grenville's experience had been considerable, and it had been of the latter kind. When he met Lady Evelyn Standish he had divined almost instantly a number of minute things which, as a woman, distinctly marked her character. She was not a woman by whom the majority of men would be attracted, or any man for mere purposes of amusement; nor would men in general, as men, have much attraction for her. He saw all this in her eyes, almost as soon as he looked at them. Frank and friendly as they were, they would never expand or soften, except under the influence of a feeling which, though she might not understand it, sprang from the very depths of her life, and would not be excited readily. His instinct taught him thus much; but it did not teach him one thing, which before very long his surprised observation did; and this was that a feeling of precisely the kind in question had, if signs meant anything, been excited in her by himself. What made him confident that his observation did not deceive him, was no vanity on his part, but his complete belief in her genuineness: and in thinking of what had happened, he was touched rather than flattered. He had, as he confessed in his diary, soon begun to experience a strong inclination to develop and return her feeling: but until he had explained himself to her guardian he had simply kept this in check; and after the explanation his part had become a delicate one. Unauthorized as yet to make to her any distinct advances, fearful of trifling with her affection, and equally fearful of chilling it, he had endeavored to maintain with her a kind of balanced relationship, which might either be warmed into love or allowed to fade into friendship. The virtual request indeed which his conduct had to convey, and to convey in such a way that she should feel rather than know its meaning, was simply this, if put into vulgar language—"Give me the refusal of you till I see if I can make you an offer." Everything, however, in such cases, depends for its ease or difficulty on the precise characters and temperaments of the two persons concerned; and Grenville felt that the character and the temperament of Lady Evelyn made a situation almost simple, which many women would have made impossible. He believed her inclination for himself to be quite sufficiently deep to obviate, for a time, at all events, any danger of a rival; and yet to be so placid that, should such a fate be in store for it, it would die of a gradual decline, without serious pain. He had had, therefore, up to the present juncture, very good if not very apparent reasons for trusting that as soon as he could ask her, she would be his for the trouble of asking; though it must be admitted that his trust owed part of its tranquillity to the fact that passion was here hardly strong enough to amuse itself with inflicting on him its customary doubts as to its object. But now, though passion had nothing to do with the change, his tranquillity began to be disturbed, and to give place to anxiety. The more he thought on the subject as the train went rumbling on, the more did this anxiety grow on him; and it filled him at last with a fever of impatient longing to be face to face with the lady without a day's unnecessary delay, and to be taking steps to dispose of his doubts forever.

Morning was gray, on the dewy pavements of Vienna as he drove to the Hotel Imperial. Could he have done so, he would have gone at once to the Embassy, to see if Lord Solway's promised letter had arrived. Exhaustion, however, gave him enough philosophy to submit to the comforts of sleep and a spring mattress; and before he was up the expected letter was brought to him. It was short, and much to the point. "My sister and her daughters," said Lord Solway, "leave for Paris to-night; and will arrive at Vicenza—you will be good enough to pay attention to dates—three days from now. They will remain there for the inside of a week, as they are going to try to get for me some chimney-pieces and doors in a certain dismantled palace. I saw them two years ago, but the price asked was exorbitant, and I had no time to bargain. My sister is going to attempt it for me; and I told her this—that I had asked you, as I knew you were coming that way, to join her if possible, and help her in her negotiations. This should reach you in time to give you one day's grace for preparations; but if you are to catch them, you must be off the morning after. I inclose you a photograph of young Oliver Jackson, with his spectacles in one hand, and Aristotle's Ethics in the other. If you like the look of him, you may perhaps meet him at Venice. He will not be at Vicenza."

No news in certain respects, except perhaps this last item, could have been more welcome to Grenville: but then came the thought of the poor old helpless relative to whose assistance he felt bound to repair. Pictures of her distress had been continually haunting his mind, and had confirmed him in his opinion that he must go to London instantly. And now it happened that if he should do so, his own opportunity would be lost. Suddenly he saw a way, and a simple way, out of the difficulty. Springing out of bed, he wrote a note to his bankers, to tell them that he might have presently to overdraw his account, which, as on a former occasion they doubtless would let him do. He then wrote a check for a hundred pounds, and inclosed it to his man of business, for his aunt's immediate relief, promising if possible to be in London the following week, and in any case to provide such further sums as might be necessary.

With Lord Solway's letter another had arrived from the Embassy—a line written by the Ambassadress, begging him to come to luncheon. His own plans being as far as possible settled, he longed for distraction, and accepted the invitation gladly. It seemed that Vienna still must be full of English, for he found his hostess surrounded by a party of English acquaintances. His various greetings over he realized that all about him questions and scraps of information were passing each other like pellets, most of them having reference to people and things at home—to the newest airs and the newest tiara of somebody, to somebody's last ball, and the people who were not invited, and to somebody's new wealth and accession to royal favor. According to superior persons all such conversation is contemptible; Grenville, however, was by no means of this opinion. He knew that rarer qualities are required for good gossip than for most of the earnest discussions by which superior persons improve themselves; and that which he heard now was as sparkling as gossip could be. But familiar as the sound of it was to him, and keenly as he would once have appreciated it, it seemed to him now like a sound heard in a dream. There was an unreality and a flatness in it he could not at all account for. He did, indeed, by an effort, laugh and talk as usual; but nothing roused in him any real interest, till he heard of the latest romance, and the latest scandal of Vienna; and this was the infatuation of the married King of Moldavia for a young unmarried girl—the new beauty of the season, who had shocked society by the audacity with which she had encouraged him, and she proved to be none other than Miss Juanita Markham. Among the company were two of the most amusing women in London, both of them amusing by their wit, and one by her absurdity also. But he only wondered now how he could ever have been entertained by either. For a moment he thought better of them, when they began to talk to him about Hungary; but he presently found this topic less inspiriting than any, because it made him long to be back again in the scenes he had just quitted.

Returning to his hotel, discontented he knew not why, he learnt from Fritz, who had been devoting himself to a study of timetables, that the journey to Vicenza would occupy thirty hours, and that if he wished to arrive on the day he had specified, the best thing he could do was to start by the express that evening. He hailed the intelligence with delight. He felt that were he only moving—moving to meet the event on which his future depended, and the woman who he hoped would share it, his discontent would vanish, and the colors of life grow bright again. He found that experience hardly confirmed his anticipations. All night and all the following day, he felt himself hourly getting nearer to the arbitress of his fate. He was pleased with the sense that he was not wasting a moment; and that no doubt was good so far as it went; but he felt that the occasion ought to have caused more stir in him, and he became depressed and puzzled by finding that he was not exhilarated.

How his condition was affected by what took place at Vicenza will be best described hereafter in his own words. It will be enough for the present to say that having remained there several days, he had left under circumstances which, to judge by his face and bearing, had not indeed elated him, or freed him from all anxiety, but had still afforded him some ground for satisfaction; and now, with no companion excepting his faithful servant, he was enjoying one pleasure at all events, which had not failed him. He was standing in the colonnade of a pale Italian villa, which stretched its frontage on the side of a low hill, and overlooked the sea-like Venetian plain. This was a villa whose name had been long familiar to him; it was one of Palladio's masterpieces, and it occurred to him on leaving Vicenza that now was his time to visit it. It was twenty miles from a town, and this enhanced its charm for him; but it had also obliged him to rise at five o'clock in the morning, in order to catch a train on a branch line, which brought him as far as a small neighboring village. The consequence was that there was still a rawness in the air, and a mist that smelt of fields and of damp vineyards, and that touched his forehead and stirred his thoughts refreshingly. He had just been through the principal range of rooms. The stuccoed exterior and the ragged grass plots in front of it had disappointed him; but the moment he entered disappointment gave place to wonder. Every foot of wall and ceiling, in the smallest ante-chamber, no less than in the largest hall, was covered with gorgeous frescoes—the work of Paul Veronese. The shining floors reflected antique Venetian furniture. Furniture and frescoes alike were perfect, and untouched by time. As Grenville stood, gazing at the distant levels, out of which here and there rose a tall, solitary campanile, he suddenly ejaculated, "What a fool I am! I declare that never occurred to me. Fritz," he shouted. "Come here. I want to speak to you. You know in my rooms in London the picture—the Paul Veronese—that hangs usually above the sideboard. Was that left on the wall, or was it locked up in the cupboard where I keep my papers?" Fritz replied, as if owning to some negligence, that it was left on the wall: but no reproof was inflicted on him. On the contrary, his master muttered to himself with complacence, "That then settles everything. Agnew a month ago offered me five hundred pounds for it. Before a week is over he shall have lodged that at my bankers. I can settle my business without going back to London. And now—now—at least for another month, wherever my wishes draw me, I am free to follow them."

CHAPTER IX.

THE white houses and the emerald leafage of Lichtenbourg had the glow on them of a warm, pearl-colored sunset. Only ten days had elapsed since Grenville and Mrs. Schilizzi had listened together to the music of the evening band, but in that short interval the rapid spring had been busy. It had multiplied leaf and blossom; it had made the flower beds glitter; and it had also called into existence a number of new visitors. It was not a number that by any means amounted to a crowd, but it still was sufficient to give an air of life to the place; and the walks and seats in the square on which the restaurant opened were gay with a sprinkling of company looking forward to dinner. There were at least a dozen exceedingly pretty dresses, and some officers in uniform ready to scrutinize and admire them; while the prettiest dress of all, surmounted by the prettiest hat, lit up the seat which was most open to observation, and shared it with an officer whose good fortune was widely envied. The officer himself evidently considered it enviable, and was making the most of his voice and his handsome eyes, while the eyes of his companion and the delicate color in her cheeks seemed to show that she was excited, even if not pleased, by the situation. He was talking to her alternately in French and German; and he was just in the middle of a quotation from a French song, which, to judge from his manner, he considered extremely telling.

> Qui veut ouïr, qui veut savior
> Comment les diplomats aiment.

"Ils aiment," he was continuing with an insinuating smile, "ils aiment si diplomatiquement," when he saw to his mortification the lady's eyes wander, and her whole expression all of a sudden change. Then she rose from the seat, and went forward abstractedly to meet a man who had suddenly stopped in front of them. This man's expression, too, as well as that of the lady, was troubled with a change, or rather with a succession of changes. Pleasure, surprise, and a something that was not pleasure, succeeded each other on his face, and remained there mixed together. As the two greeted each other, a very acute observer might have seen that their cordiality, or at least its extreme openness, was in part due to nervousness quite as much as to feeling. The officer, however, was far from being acute; and having borne neglect heroically for the better part of a minute, he rose, lit a cigar, and catching the eye of the lady, while pique shone in his own, he gallantly forced a smile, made a bow and departed. Had he waited a moment longer, he would not, perhaps, have fled so precipitately; for the manner of the lady and her friend, when the first greeting was over, grew rapidly more constrained, and almost suggested coldness.

"Do you know, Mr. Grenville, I was never so surprised in my life," the lady was saying. "I thought you must have been your ghost."

"Well," he answered, "and I really believe I might have been, for since I saw you I have been through a kind of death. My dear Mrs. Schilizzi, you needn't look so concerned. If I told you my meaning you would say, 'Is it only that?'"

"Well," she laughed, "at all events that's a comfort; but what you said had a most tragic sound in it. I thought you were in England."

"I have managed," he said, "to settle my business without going there; and I have done now what, if possible, I always meant to do. I have come back here to see the castle whose photograph we were looking at at luncheon the day when I last saw you. It seems a year ago to me—that does, so much has happened since then."

"To me, too, it seems ages."

"Is that," he said, "because so much has happened to you too?"

"It is rather," she replied, "because nothing has."

She had not resumed her seat. They were walking together slowly. They were silent for a few moments; and then with a constrained indifference, "You have, at any rate, found," he said, "a very attentive acquaintance."

She looked up at him with a half mischievous smile. "What?" she asked, "do you mean that Austrian captain? I met him at Vienna at a public ball last year. Perhaps he is, now that you come to mention it, one of the things that has made my time pass slowly. He's handsome, and would be pleasant if he'd never open his mouth. As it is, he's been boring my very life out; and the only pleasure he's given me is the thought that he goes to-morrow."

At this news Grenville's expression softened. He

asked her where she dined. She told him in her own rooms, adding that she had letters to write, and would not reappear that evening.

"Then, perhaps," said Grenville, "I shall see you to-morrow morning. Will you let me tell you my adventures? And if we find it can be managed, perhaps you will make another expedition with me?"

"I can never," she said, "see you in the morning. Quite early, I have to see after my children; and then for some time I am busy with something of my own. In spite of the charm of your friend, the Austrian officer, I have been obliged to make an occupation for many hours of solitude."

"And what occupation is that?" he asked.

"I wonder," she said, "if I can tell you; you'll only laugh if I do. What do you think it is? I have begun writing a diary."

"I too not long since began doing the same thing. I daresay we're not singular. My diary, I find, has one merit at all events; my last few days in Italy have turned it into a book of surprises."

"Italy!" she exclaimed. "And have you been in Italy? I should like to hear about that. One of these days you will perhaps tell me—that is to say if you are not going directly. Good-by, it is late—I must be going in to my children."

As she said this they were just at the entrance of the hotel; and, without giving him time to detain her by some question which she saw was on his lips, she ran up the steps, throwing a parting smile at him, and was lost to sight in the shadow within the doorway.

Grenville was not much pleased by this abrupt ending

of the interview; and after dinner he loitered in the neighborhood of the band, hoping that after all she should find a chance of renewing it. But he looked in vain for her. She had been quite sincere in saying that the whole of that evening she meant to give to her letters; and she was, indeed, in her sitting-room with envelopes and paper before her. These, however, she presently pushed aside. "I can't write," she murmured, and drawing toward her some sheets of foolscap, she began, not to write, but to read something already written to them. This was the beginning of her diary.

What she read was as follows:

"Different people write diaries for different reasons and objects; some because they do so much else, others because they have so little else to do; some to record what they have seen, others to record what they have *been*. As for me, the last case is mine. I have done nothing and seen nothing. What have I *been* is my only history. And why am I going to write it—or try to write it? Not because I am idle, but because I am lonely, and I must speak to something—I must be myself somehow. I write for the same sort of reason that makes a boy sing, or a woman at times sob. Just as a sob relieves the heart, so will this writing relieve something else in me—something—I don't know what.

"But before I regularly begin, I want to assure myself of one thing—that I am not like a silly, sentimental schoolgirl, sighing and crying over her own fancies. I have known some girls—girls who have kept diaries, and who have used them like looking-glasses in which they made interesting faces at themselves. I am not like that; I wish to see myself as I am and have been; and

I shall try to record this, and I believe I shall be able to do so. I don't know life, but I do at least know my own life, uneventful as it must seem to every human being that has known me. Its events have been all within. I know the difference between fact and fancy; but I do not know the difference between fact and feeling. There are facts which are not feelings, but all feelings are facts, and the only facts which give the others any meaning. What would action be if it affected nobody's feelings? It might as well be something taking place in Jupiter. What would thought be if we felt nothing? Thought at its highest is but the genius—the slave of the lamp, which either guides feeling or works for it.

"Yes, but granting all this, here comes another question which will trouble me till I have made my answer to it. My life may consist of facts, even though it only consists of feelings. But are they facts worth having their history written? Will my sense of the ridiculous allow me to think they are? Yes—yet, it will, and for this reason. Every human body may not be a good model to draw, but every human body would be a good subject to dissect—how much more every human soul! Who am I? what am I? I am nobody, and less than nothing. I am not even one of my own few possibilities. I know it. And yet if human existence has any meaning at all, my life must have some meaning also. None of us is worth anything, if any one of us is not worth something.

"How philosophical I am! But I am going to be philosophical no longer. I sink, with a sudden fall, to the style of a foolish woman.

"I call this a diary. It will at first be a memoir, for I

can only get at myself by going first back to my childhood. The chief characteristic of my life I can trace in it even then—that I was alone. My own mind was my only real playground. I do not mean that I was an only child, or that in any marked way I isolated myself from my brothers and sisters. On the contrary, I laughed and romped and lay in the hay, and climbed trees with them. But as I dangled my legs from the boughs—I remember it still so clearly—what filled my consciousness was the world of leafy branches and the green lights which seemed, in some strange way, to hint to me of another life. When I lay among the hay and looked up at the sky, the clouds were enchanted mountains, and I wandered among their dissolving passes.

"How often have I heard people say that self-analysis is morbid! But what I am writing now is not self-analysis; I only wish it was; I wish that myself then were myself now. Oh, little girl who are lost, who never can live again, I can think about you and describe you as if you were someone else. The sole link between us is the nerve called memory—that is so often aching—and the pronoun 'I.'

"And yet, perhaps, I am wrong. As I write on, I shall see.

"My father and mother were both people of family, though they never mixed in what is commonly called the world; but in both their characters was a certain pride, which, though we were not important enough for it to develop in us exclusiveness, did develop something which is nearly the same—seclusiveness. All my childhood was spent in an inclosed garden.

"And what sort of childhood was it? I have said

something about it already; but not all I want to say. In going on I feel a kind of diffidence. It is easy enough to say that my life was a life of loneliness, but it is not so easy to say—at least I shrink from doing so— that the heart of that loneliness was religion. But so it was. Nobody would have thought so, and clergymen would not admit that I am using the word rightly. For I do not mean that I was always going to church, or always or indeed often saying my prayers; but I was full of the longing that moves people to pray, and to do and feel many other things besides. It was a longing for something beyond and above me, and at the same time about me, but always eluding me. I saw it in the sky and in the woods, and I heard it in church when the organ sounded. As for what people commonly call religion, I had to pick up my knowledge of it pretty much for myself, for mother was born a Catholic, though she went to the English church; and my father, though a very good man, had, I believe, only one religious belief, and this was that the Church of Rome was wrong. Still I was confirmed; and when I went to my first communion, I felt—I can't express it now; how it was something the same feeling I had when first I saw the sea; or when the sky, or a flower, or anything, struck me suddenly with its depth of beauty. I remember so well how on such occasions I used sometimes to whisper to myself 'How beautiful!' and sometimes 'God be good to me!' It was a chance which of the two I whispered; I meant the same by both.

"I remember also another thing, which makes me laugh as I think of it. I used often—as most girls do— to stand looking at myself in the glass; and the beauty of my own reflection, such as it was, moved me and troubled me, much as other beauty did. I never thought —never, so far as I can remember, 'There's beautiful me.' I only thought 'There's a beautiful something.' I seemed to myself, as I looked at my cheeks, to be merely like a flower given into my own keeping, and I wondered about the meaning of the petals, and was half frightened at their delicacy.

"Idiot that I am to write these trifles down! And yet am I? They are facts—hard, unvarnished facts of a life that at all events was quite free from affectations. And why should the movements of a young girl's thoughts not be as well worth recording as the movements of sap in a vegetable?

"Anyhow I have put enough of them down now. I go on to what is broader. All these feelings of mine, for the sky, the sea, for church music, or my own complexion, were only manifestations of a constant something within me, panting to fulfill itself, and not knowing how.

"But, though it did not know, it was always trying to find out; and these attempts form really the whole history of my girlhood. Poetry, drawing, music, and then knowledge—hard, dry knowledge—I tried them all. I am not talking of what I did in the schoolroom—that counts for nothing. I am talking only of what I did by myself, and with my whole heart prompting me. And indeed everything that came home to me I had to pick up in this way, much as I did by instruction about religion, without any help or guidance. What volumes of poetry at one time I knew by heart! I found them all out for myself, and took to them only because I hoped to find in them some answer to the question 'What is it that I long for?' But they did not quiet me, they only made me more restless; and I felt an impulse to do—to fulfill myself by action. I tried to draw and paint, and till I saw I could do neither, for a good six months I was almost beside myself with hope. Then I think came music. Could I only have done what I attempted, the music of the spheres would have been nothing to what I should have extracted from a cottage piano. But the keys at last became like a row of tombstones, forming a cemetery in which my attempts were buried. After that I began to read books of science and philosophy, full of hard words the meaning of which I had to guess at; and it seemed to me for a considerable time that what I longed for, was to be found in the satisfaction of the intellect. What ideas I had! How my mind rode away on them and if they were wings! I used to work them out in things that I called essays, trembling with pride as I wielded the long words of Mr. Herbert Spencer. And then generally, by the time I had read a little more, I found all the profundities I had arrived at were mere truisms or commonplaces, or that else they were nonsense. But I was not discouraged—at least not for a long time. Perhaps—perhaps—I am not wholly discouraged now. If I am, I am done for.

"And all this while, what became of my religion—I mean my religion of prayers and church-going? I can't quite tell. The whole history of it is so vague. The fact is, about such matters I was not very clear to begin with; and with me, feeling, and faith, and longing, and self-prostration, were so much more than any defined beliefs, that I hardly noticed how these last were gradually sapped by the books which I read so eagerly, and how so much of what the clergyman said came gradually to seem so foolish. But I think it was only the words that I heard in Church that lost their power over me. I put these aside as one might put aside the libretto of an opera which had some connection with the music, but only an insufficient one; while the meaning of the music itself still remained the same for me, and shook my heart as the organ shook the windows. How often contrition—I can't tell for that—came trembling into me, and the spirit of prayer bowed me, as the wind bends corn! But what came oftenest was mere adoration—mere longing—again I can't tell for what: but all was for the same thing that I felt in nature, that I tried to capture in drawing, and to express in music, and to find in thought and study. Some people, who lose any of the definite beliefs which they learnt as children, experience much misery at the loss. I don't think I did; and the reason was what I have just stated—that the definite part of religion was to me the least important part. Indeed I remember saying to myself one day in church, when the clergyman was preaching about Joshua's moon in Ajalon, 'Perhaps I have not got a religion; but I myself *am* religion.' I meant, 'I am longing for whatever will most completely fulfill myself,' and my only articulate prayer was little more than this—'Reveal to me what I long for, and unite me completely with it.'

"If anyone besides myself were to read these confessions, I know one thing which he or she would say—'This silly girl in search of an object for her sentiment—did it never occur to her to fancy herself in love? Did she never try to solve her perplexities that way?' Yes and no—but much more no than yes. Love did enter into my thoughts; but let me explain how. I felt myself capable of it; but I felt this in some far-off way. As for associating the idea of it with anyone I ever met, that seemed to me sacrilege. I felt it to be something which was so sacred, and which, if it came, would be so overwhelming, that it frightened me. It made me afraid of myself, as if I held within me some mystery. One or two men—indeed more than one or two, while I was still quite young, fell in love with me. Instead of being flattered or touched by this, I felt it as a kind of impertinence, and I was glad when I saw how very easily I could repulse them. They, I believe, thought I was heartless. I was not. It was because I reverenced my heart so much, and felt in such awe of the Unknown contained in it, that I was indignant at them for presuming to think about it. Could I only love—this is the thought that would come to me—what would the feeling be? I should die of it. Where would it carry me? I was afraid to go on thinking. I only knew this, that I never had seen anyone, and could not imagine anyone, who would justify the feeling in me, and make it not seem wicked. I remember it still—how afraid I grew of myself. I hardly dared even, at one time, to read Keats's poetry, it moved me so, without any justifying cause.

"The only emotion, the only love, that I could indulge in frankly, and that supported and did not frighten me, was love of my parents. They didn't understand me—I always felt that; but I felt that they desired my welfare; and though they could not share my thoughts, it seemed to me that they sheltered them. What was my pain then when one day quite by accident, I heard mother saying this to father—'Irma is so pretty, that she ought to marry well.' And then, before I could get out of hearing, I caught the name of a neighboring country squire. I had no dislike to the man—I thought nothing about him; but to hear him mentioned in this way, was like hearing a knife talked about that was to be drawn across my throat. After that, for three weeks I was miserable. Father and mother couldn't tell what had come to me, and when a letter arrived from my aunt, asking me to stay with her in Hungary, they thought the change would be good for me, and gladly let me go. It was arranged that a friend of my aunt who was going there at the same time, should look after me on the journey. I knew nothing of him, till I saw him, except his name and the fact that he was very rich; and after I had seen him, I knew nothing more for weeks, except that he had almond-shaped dark eyes, a straight nose, and a smile; that he talked rather fast, and that he talked a great deal to me. My aunt told me that if he had wished it the Emperor would have made him a baron. A few days later she told me he wished to marry me.

"How I consented I really can hardly tell. Secret correspondence went on between my aunt and my parents; and mother wrote to me and told me how happy my prospects were, and how little money I should ever have of my own; and how sad and anxious she had once been for my future. One reason, I think, why I at length yielded, one reason why I did not shrink from this marriage as I might have done, was just the very fact that for me there was no love in it. Marriage came to me as something completely outside myself; it came to me simply as a new shell of circumstance, into which, with unavowed pressure, mother and all the others pushed me.

How could I know what I was doing, or what was being done to me? I had no experience.

"Well, I have experience now. And yet who would think it? No one who had watched me or lived with me, no matter how constantly or closely. Who could guess the history of my first married years? Certainly not my husband; and for one very sufficient reason, he never would care to try. My brother Robert told me how, when he first went to school, he used to cry to himself at nights, longing for home, thinking with a passionate affection of every worn patch in the carpets, and of the air full of peace and tenderness. For three years after my marriage I did just the same. I had plenty of servants, and an extravagant cook: but every time I looked at our smart dinner-table I thought of our schoolroom meals—our broiled mutton—our rice pudding; and I longed like a truant to run away and go back to them. What would mother have thought if she had seen me come back to her, and hiding, as I should have liked to hide, my face once more in her lap!

"What could I have told her? How could I have explained such a step? I could not have explained it in any intelligible way to her. I could indeed have summed up my experience in a very few words. I could have said to her, Marriage is the suicide of hope; but I could tell her no facts that would explain so tragic a view. I could have told her that Paul's temper was not always, or often, of the best. In fact when I made mistakes in any little household matters, he was furious with me; and once, though I must say he was handsomely sorry for it afterward, he struck me on the wrist with an ivory paper knife, leaving a mark which for a fortnight I hid with a velvet band. I didn't mind that. Indeed I think the only time that I ever voluntarily kissed Paul was after he had struck me, just to show that I had forgiven him. No—what I minded was not what he was, but the sense which he inflicted on me daily of what he was not. He liked me in a way. In a way he took good care of me. But the way was this: he regarded me as a piece of china, which ornamented his drawing-room, and which had to be dusted carefully. The only difference between me and an *epergne* he was very proud of, was that it stood in the middle of the table, and I sat at the end of it. I was like a book which he valued for the rarity of its binding, but which he neither could nor cared to read. How long I hoped against hope that this might not be true— that he was merely shy, merely slow in understanding me, and that we should at last really become companions! I tried to love him, and to make him love me, and could I only have met with any response from him, to some extent at least, I should have succeeded. I tried every means I could think of. In the afternoon I used to hurry home, in order to meet him when he returned from the railway he was then making. I did all I could to look glad and happy when I saw him. But the only result was this. Five minutes after I was in the drawing-room he was sure to go out of it; and if ever I ventured to follow him into his study, he invariably met me by asking me what I wanted. What did I want? It makes me laugh now to think of his asking that of me. It was something, Paul, you could never have understood, if I had told you. But at dinner, Paul, you couldn't rebuff me for being with you; and do you remember how I tried then to find my way into your life? I tried at first to talk about the things that interested me or touched me—about the things that seemed to me to be beautiful, or happy, or sad, or perplexing. Good heavens! I might have been talking Hebrew to you. I put my thoughts into your hands—thoughts which I valued and cherished; and I hoped that you might be pleased with them. But what you did was to stare at them blankly, and then drop them, and let them break themselves into pieces. But still I would not be disheartened. I tried to approach you in another way. As you would not talk to me about my subjects, I tried to talk to you about yours. That annoyed you still more. It made you rude to me, not only cold. How different you were with men—with the men you brought to dine with you! They and you understood each other. You responded to what they said to you, as if you were a musical instrument touched by them—or rather a band of instruments—a band of instruments at a music hall. When I spoke to you, it was as if I was thumping on wood. To try to talk to you was like going out into a frosty day. How cold I was when I came back to myself again!

"During those three years, it seems to me that I was dead. If it had not been for my two children I should have died literally. I was very fond of them from the first; but babies are not companions. Though they were near my heart, they could not tell how it was aching. Still they kept me alive. They prevented my heart from freezing. But when the eldest began to know me, and speak and understand a little, then I was conscious of some new accession of happiness; and gradually, to my surprise, I felt in better spirits. I felt at last that I was something like myself again: and to Paul's extreme annoyance, I sang in the hall one morning. He swore at me, and I cried. No matter. What I was going to say was this. This revival of my spirits, through my growing love for my children, had a very odd effect on me. My vanity woke up again. I wanted company, I wanted a little amusement. Sometimes in the afternoon, when I was left all alone, I used to look at myself in the glass, and wish that someone could see me. I should have been quite satisfied with a woman. I should often have liked a woman best; but sometimes, I confess, I did wish for a man or two—just for the sake of seeing what effect I produced. My desire for admiration had all the temerity of innocence. That I could do anything wrong, or even wish for it, never seemed possible to me. Well—I made some acquaintances, not among Paul's connections. I made friends with some pretty and well-connected women; and through them I came to know a certain number of men. My wishes soon fulfilled themselves. Every afternoon I had some admiring visitors.

"What things in life can be more different than some of our wishes before their fulfillment and after! These men I speak of—all their attention and homage at first flattered and soothed me after Paul's neglect. Paul could never see too little of me. They could never see too much. At first this was charming. I really took an interest in some of them, and thought they did in me. But little by little, various things enlightened me. These men saw my beauty; but I now divined how they saw it; and they appeared to me hardly human. When their voices grew soft, how I hated them! And yet, in spite of this I allowed them to go on calling on me; and I began to take a sort of perverse pleasure in keeping them captive under false colors. /I sheltered my real self—the self they could never understand—under an outer husk of the false self that they imagined;/ and I thus enjoyed two different sorts of pride—one derived from their admiration of me, the other derived from my contempt for them.

"This has not been good for me; but it led to what was worse. The women with whom I now associated, and who were friends also of these men, almost before I was aware of it, made me one of their sisterhood. I thought they were angels first; and then I learnt that they were not angels. How kind and pleasant they were to me, and what torture they inflicted on me, when they first let me know them thoroughly! What they did, so far as I am concerned, was this. They did not induce me to follow their ways; but they made me familiar with their ideas. One of them lent me a number of French novels. They were novels by celebrated writers—classics; but oh, how wicked they seemed! How wicked the women were in them! I felt this, and yet I read. I read one book after another. But then after a time, I felt I could stand it no longer. Some of the books I burnt; and others, I don't know where they are.

"If anyone else—I again come back to that—if anyone else were to read what I have just written, what dreadful things he or she would think of me! I should seem to be suggesting so much more than I have said. Wrong! wrong! What I have said has been the uttermost that I mean, so far as badness and folly goes. And now I have this to add. These women, these men—their companionship and their flattery, were not all my life even then, or indeed, I think, the most important part of it. For just as my happiness in my children roused my vanity and my wish for excitement, because it raised my spirits, so did this excitement and this tribute to my vanity, revive in me other things, not by raising my spirits but by troubling them. Those dreadful novels were not the only books I read; nor was admiration the only thing I thought of. I took again to my books of science and philosophy; I bought translations of all kinds of classical writers. My old longing to realize my own existence once more took possession of me; and all the false companionship which I now got, made my mind tumultuous with longing for some companionship that should be true. As to what this true companionship would be, I was as far off as ever from knowing. Would it take the form of knowledge, of beauty, or of a human friend! I know one thing—that not once, but several times, when the best of my admirers was coming to see me, and I had promised to be in by a certain hour in the afternoon, I forgot all about him in looking at a March sunset from a lonely seat among some pine trees, more than a mile from home.

"And what am I now? How structureless all my history is. What I have just written applies to the last four or five years of my life; and applies to me at this moment. Am I fairly good? or am I very bad? Five or six men are, I know, this moment in love with me; and I have been proud to think they are so, though I have no love for them. Is not that bad? But somehow, when I think it over, it makes me feel, not how bad I am, but how lonely I am. I have never in my whole life been myself to anyone. I have so many unuttered thoughts troubling me and increasing in number. I don't know what I should have been could I only have met someone, who would have helped me to live—with whom I could have shared something beyond a part of his income and the parentage of two children—a number that never will be added to.

"Oh, you—what have you done to me! You took me—you *would* marry me. You took an entire life, and you sacrificed it, in order to ornament one small corner of your own. And I—I tried to love you. I waited for you and watched for you during your absence. I ran to meet you when you came. Your own mind was for me like waterless sand; none of my thoughts would grow in it. I found that out; and then what I tried to do was to share that desert with you, acting as if it were some kind oasis. And I would have done this had you let me. In some sort I would have learned to love you; Paul, I would have indeed done that; but you repulsed me. Do you remember that night when you struck me, and when I kissed you because I saw you were sorry? You were sorry you struck me; you were sorry you had struck a woman; you were ashamed of yourself; but not even then did you show any tenderness for me. It is not the blow I remember with any bitterness. It is what came after.

"And now, whom can I speak to? To no one. You have made me bitterly wise. You have taken even my mother from me. Not even to her can I speak with perfect confidence. You have made me feel that she sacrificed her daughter, treated her daughter as a thing without heart or soul. You have driven me into the company of waters, and woods, and sunsets. In nature I do feel a vague something that touches me, that moves in me the religious impulse, that calls me out of myself. And yet whenever I see a beautiful thing, along with the sense of its beauty, I have this sense also—that I have no one to whom I can turn, and say 'how beautiful!'

"Mother, perhaps, would tell me that I ought to make the best of things. I know she thinks I could be happy and successful socially. Could I? How little she knows. She sees me, as I too can see myself in the glass. She sees me dressed perfectly, from the hat to the tips of my shoes. She sees how certain shades of color become me. But for all that I am alone. She doesn't wish me to be bad; and I can't be worldly. Great ladies alarm me; bad women repel me. What a simple life would content me, if I could only live it!

"And yet I am ungrateful. One treasure I have, though one only—my children. They keep me alive; they prevent my soul from dying. If there is any revelation at all, my children reveal God to me. Oh, my beloved ones, let me pour out my heart to you! Let me spend and be spent for you. My little ones, forgive your mother, for I have sometimes been so selfish as this: I have wished that you might be ill and suffering, that I might wear myself out in tending you.

"And yet, my little ones, there are solitudes in your mother's heart, which you even cannot fill. She can be your companion, but in some ways you cannot be hers."

Mrs. Schilizzi, when she finished her reading, with a listless deliberation took up her pen, and though her hand trembled as she did so, she set herself to resume her writing. She tried to continue her narrative without any formal break; but having completed a sentence or two she presently scratched them out, and abandoning all attempt at literary form or consistency, she abruptly put down the date, and slowly, but without hesitation, wrote the following few lines, which might have come from the diary of a child.

"I am at Lichtenbourg now. All these pages were written here. I like it very much. It is very pretty; but, as usual, I have been alone. To my amazement, Mr. Grenville reappeared this evening, and spoke to me very kindly. I believe he is kind really. I had come to think that, when I was here with him before, he was laughing at me or amusing himself by pretending to be kind. But I don't think so now; and I am beginning to feel grateful. A very little kindness, of real kindness, quite upsets me. Oh, how my head is aching. If I think more I shall make a fool of myself. I will kiss my children, and then try to sleep. Olga, darling, darling, I shall have you by my side."

CHAPTER X.

GRENVILLE, who was bent on making his expedition to the castle, and who was anxious to secure Mrs. Schilizzi as his companion, was annoyed, as he dressed next morning, to remember her account of her occupations, and to think that it was many hours before he could hope to see her. Just, however, as he was about to leave the hotel, in order to pay an early visit to the springs, a pretty looking French maid tripped after him with a note, scribbled in pencil, and consisting of the following words: "I am not well, and shall not be writing this morning. If you can do so, will you take me for a walk at eleven?—IRMA SCHILIZZI."

Grenville was delighted, and sent back Yes for an answer. At eleven o'clock they met by the glittering kiosk. Close to this was a bed purple with violets. They both stooped to inhale the pure, delightful perfume, and they went off together as if the soul of the spring were in their pulses. As they passed through the town the entire world seemed young. Sunshine lay on all the people they came across. The little shops twinkled with their wares, as if shopkeeping were a happy-hearted play.

"Look," said Mrs. Schilizzi, as they passed a villa garden, "at the bells of the magnolias white in the blue sky!"

Grenville turned to her with a smile of half amazement.

"You know," he said, "how princes and princesses in fairy tales are transformed into cats or lions, and every kind of shape. It seems to me to-day as if happiness had been transformed into flowers."

His own happiness was such, indeed, that he had gone on walking beside her, without any thought of what direction they were taking; but realizing presently that they had left the town behind them he said to her, "Where are we going? have you any idea? I've not."

"I am taking you," she said, "to a place I've found out myself. Do you see this river which comes flowing out of the woods and valleys? We are going to turn into the footpath, which skirts it beside the willows."

They left the road, following the course she indicated. Birds sang with the water, and all the foliage whispered. At last they reached a curious timbered mill, with which was united a simple but picturesque restaurant. There was a garden containing arbors, and a large inviting summer house. "I often," said Mrs. Schilizzi, "bring my children to tea here. The woman gives them such beautiful cakes and biscuits; and early in the season, she tells me, it is always perfectly quiet. You mustn't think I do nothing but talk to Austrian officers."

They passed through the gate and seated themselves on the green benches of the summer house. "I'm a little tired," she said. "Will you order a cup of coffee for me? Last night I was restless and hardly slept at all. It would have been nice to have breakfasted here; but I must go back to my children. Ah!" she went on, when the coffee was brought out to her, "how peaceful this place is! Will you tell me, while we rest, for you have not told me yet—what you have seen in Italy, and why you have returned to Lichtenbourg?"

They had attempted during their walk no serious conversation; they had both been content with merely being happy together, and the consequence was they were now quietly at their ease with each other.

"I wonder," Grenville answered, "if you believe in mesmerism. Mesmerists, it is said, can make their subjects come back to them at a specified time, and no matter from what distance. I believe that old castle, whose picture the princess showed us, must have mesmerized me and brought me back here. It is only ten miles away. You think I am laughing at you; I see that in your face. But I am not, only——"

"Only what?"

"The question you asked me sounded a very simple one, but to answer it truly, do you know what I should have to inflict on you? A long discourse on the philosophy of life generally—especially upon prose and poetry, and the types of life that correspond to them."

"Go on," she said, starting with surprise and pleasure. "This is what I like listening to."

He hesitated a little as if doubtful how to express himself. "You know," he began, "how all our modern philosophers denounce as useless the life of the contemplative monastic orders. Virtue they say is utility, not private perfection. But to Christian critics, at all events, the monks and nuns have an answer. Different people have different works in the world; theirs is to be a complete realization of certain spiritual possibilities, which every Christian should try to realize partially. Well, what the saints are for men as Christians, the poets are for men as men. The highest use of the ordinary career of action, is to improve the conditions of living. The use of the poet is to illustrate, to reveal, or to enlarge the resources of life itself. Do you see my meaning?"

"Yes," she said eagerly, "of course I do."

"I talk of poets," he continued, "but I didn't mean merely people who write verses. I mean people whose preponderating desire is to live the life of which poetry is the articulate expression. Poetry is merely the body of which those who appreciate it are the soul. Few people can write good love poems, but whoever loves deeply, lives one."

"Go on," she murmured, "your words are like carrier pigeons. My feelings have wings, but my words can hardly flutter."

"A new poet," he said, "is like a new spring, making new flowers grow in the human mind; but they must have been sleeping there beforehand. I am not thinking specially of love, but of every kind of feeling that fills the mind with music, or lifts it with aspiration. Think of Shelley and Goethe, and then of Napoleon and the Duke of Wellington. Compared with a campaign or a revolution, what a foolish thing a poem seems! And yet all that makes life worth fighting for is the jewels that the poets brighten. I am obliged to say all this, as you will see presently, in order to defend myself from my own self-criticisms. Let me tell you what I think is the true definition of poetry. It is the emotional expression of a sense of life's value, or else of disappointment at not finding in it a value it once was thought to have. I don't mean that a poem need be all sentiment. Poems like 'Faust' and 'Hamlet' may be full of profoundest thought:

but thought in poetry is always thought which is indirect connection with emotion: and that emotion, whatever it may be, depends upon some belief in the value and the beauty of life. Well, such being the case, I put the matter in this way. ⎣Poetry is religion secularized;⎦ and the poetic life, or, if you like to call it so, the romantic life, is the monastic life secularized. You may say that in one sense it is useless; but it embodies and keeps up an idea just as truly as the life of a monastic body vowed to perpetual adoration. What are you listening to? The clock? Yes—it is striking twelve."

"We must go," she said, "my children breakfast in half an hour. Don't stop what you are saying. Finish it as we walk back."

"A love-match," he resumed as soon as they were on their way—"I mean a marriage which has nothing but love to recommend it, is an attempt at the poetic life, even if it is not always an attainment of it. Most people—and in most cases they are right—think such a marriage ridiculous. The reason is that the lovers in most cases have not a true vocation. You see," he went on, picking up a stone and jerking it into the river, and speaking in a matter-of-fact voice as if he were reading an advertisement out of the *Times*, "the need for this kind of life varies in intensity in different natures. But I believe, though I have never been fortunate enough to prove the belief by experience, that for some people who find affection, and who leave for its sake houses and lands and ambition, the heavens are opened as truly as they were for Stephen."

They were both silent for a time, not from any sense of embarrassment, but merely because respectively they were following out their own thoughts. At last she said gently, "But Stephen's vision was a dream."

"Yes," said Grenville, "and what higher end could there be for all practical activity, for all public careers, for all social reforms, than to make beds for all of us on which to dream dreams like these?"

Again there was silence which presently he interrupted with a laugh. She looked at him nervously and asked him what amused him. "Merely to think," he said, "how far I must seem to have strayed from the question you asked me—why I came back to Lichtenbourg. Well, what we have just been saying, will help me to tell you why. I have no vocation for the high poetic life. My lot is cast among prose, and labor, and ambition. But the poetic life still at times has charms for me; and I long to escape to that happy world of the imagination, where those for whom love and romance bear no direct message, can follow and hear their echoes in all the valleys of the past. That world of the imagination I now find in this country. This country to me happens to represent poetry; it liberates me from the limitations of my circumstances. Italy last week represented prose. That is why I have come back here. I am like a schoolboy who has run home from school. Do you understand all this nonsense?"

"Yes," she said, "yes. I didn't answer you because I'm thinking about it. Of course," she went on presently, "people must act and work. Goethe said that action is the cure of doubt; but it seems to me that it is the cure of aspiration also. I only speak for myself. I want, personally, not to act, but to be. That is the reason why I was so interested in what you said about saints and poets. Poetry, the sense of beauty, and the aspiration for something beyond, which comes from the sense of beauty as the scent comes from a flower—you say that this is religion secularized. I should be content to say simply that it is religion; and I should wish if I knew how, to lead the religious life. I sometimes think it is wicked to feel like this—that it is wishing to be selfish and useless; but you have reassured me a little. Besides, when a woman"— she said this slowly and softly—"when a woman says that she wishes not to act but to be, her real wish, I suppose, is to be something for the sake of somebody else. I want to be something, for instance, for the sake of my children. They are my religion—or at least the practical part of it. The next service will be their breakfast or luncheon. Will you take part in it? If you will, you will be very welcome; and you will see what I think is a real triumph of management—that I have got the *chef* to make me a genuine child's rice pudding."

He was not only pleased but touched by this homely invitation. As he entered her salon with her, where the cloth was already laid, she said to him, "Mr. Grenville, you will think I am very stupid. I am so, I know; but with you I seem more stupid than I am. You keep me silent by giving me so much to think of."

Had she made such a speech to him when first he began to know her, he would have certainly tried to acknowledge it with some species of compliment. But now the stage of compliments seemed to have passed away; and his only answer was: "No, you are not stupid." The children rushed to their mother, like flowers opening in the sun; and then turning to Grenville, who had played with them when they were staying with the Princess, they gave him a share of the smiles which their mother had called into existence. A sense of partnership with her subtly stole into his heart and spread its enchantment over the whole simple meal. This was deepened from time to time by the gentle unconscious way in which she asked him to do this or that for the children, as if he were a friend whom she might call on for all assistance; and through all his present consciousness echoes of their morning's conversation made a vibrating music and the ripple of the river sang to him.

The children had a passion for flowers; and asked Grenville, who told them he had seen quantities in the meadows, why he had not brought them some. "Suppose," he said, turning to Mrs. Schilizzi, "that we have tea at the mill. They can, as we go, pick flowers to their heart's content." The proposal was received by the children with exclamations of delight, and the mother's eyes had assented even before her lips did. "Let us go at five," she said, "till then it is too hot."

"In that case," said Grenville, "hot as it is, I will fill up the time between by a visit I have been meaning to pay—a visit to Count T——, to whom I have an introduction, and who no doubt will tell us something about the country."

The count's castle, perched on its wooded eminence, could be reached on foot by a climb of half an hour. Grenville's visit was in every way satisfactory; and when he rejoined his friends and went off to the mill with them, he was full of accounts of what he had heard and seen. "The castle," he said, "of which the Princess told us, can be reached from here easily; and the Count declares it is really the most curious sight in the country. He was particularly anxious also that I should go to a place of his own—an hotel which he has built in the heart of one of his forests, near a lake and a mineral spring, and which is going to be opened presently. He has a hunting lodge close by, which, if I cared for fishing, he said would be at my disposal for as long as I chose to occupy it. Suppose one day we accept this handsome offer, so far as to drive over there, and use the lodge for a picnic."

They were sitting in the summer house, the scene of their morning's talk, hearing the mill wheel turn with its plunging murmur, and watching the children as they went to and fro like butterflies. Presently, at the gate of the garden appeared an itinerant flute player, who began some simple melody, the notes of which were sweet as a thrush's. The children dropped their flowers, and ran off to listen to him. Mrs. Schilizzi, pleased with the scene before her, seemed pleased still farther at the idea of the proposed expedition. Seeing this Grenville continued, "I have something else to propose besides. The castle we were speaking of belongs to a Baron K——, who has two rooms in it, which he occupies for a week sometimes; and he is, the Count tells me, expected there in a day or two. While he is in residence, the castle is closed to strangers. So what do you say? Do you think you would have the energy to take time by the forelock, and go there with me to-morrow?"

"Listen to the flute," she said. "To-day has been full of music. To go to the castle would make to-morrow full of it also. Find out about getting there, and this evening I will tell you if I can manage it."

He met her at the band, after dinner. They stayed there for a short time only. The scene struck both of them as artificial, after their late experiences; but he sat with her long enough to convince her that the expedition was an easy one, and when he said good-night to her she had agreed to undertake it with him. It was too long for the children, so she stipulated for a late start, which would leave them their mother's company for nearly all the morning. An hour's drive and half an hour in the train, brought them to a station almost at the foot of the castle. It was a station which stood among flat fields and furrows, and all around were hills covered with forest. Here and there some peasant women were working; the roads were nothing but primitive unfenced tracks; silence and sunshine slept on the whole country. And straight before them, rising from the quiet levels, was a spire of rock, covered with wood, and gleaming with roofs and turrets.

Mrs. Schilizzi gave an exclamation of delight. "You are better than your word," she said. "This is indeed a country of romance."

Near as the castle was—they seemed to be almost under it—they had before them harder work than they bargained for. The beginning of the ascent was up some grassy slopes, which brought them at last to a grove of ragged pine trees; and here, gray among the foliage, they discovered a moss-grown tower. Passing through this by a gateway, they found themselves on a rising road, with a battlemented wall on the outer side, and impending precipices on the inner—a road which wound upward round the rock like a corkscrew. At every fifty yards they came to a fresh tower, with an iron door and a moldering coat-of-arms, and now and then to a gap spanned by a creaking drawbridge. The ascent was so steep and long, and the whole scene was so singular that they often paused, at once to rest and to think. Down below there were the fields at an increasing depth; up in the air were the walls and gables of the castle. Even Fritz, who had accompanied them, was overcome with the spectacle, and said to his master, "Sir, if these trees could talk, what strange things they would tell!" As for Grenville and Mrs. Schilizzi, they hardly spoke at all. He at first had made one or two observations; but she presently said, "Don't talk. I feel as if I were in a cathedral." They were conscious, however, of thinking the same thoughts; and by and by, seeing that she was growing tired, he had merely to look at her, and without thanks or apology, she took his arm, and silently leaned her weight on it.

Thus they reached the summit. Under some archways hung a smell of wood smoke; and here and there a few cocks and hens were straying. These were the first signs of life they had come across; and Fritz was sent to see if he could find the custodian. Grenville and his companion found themselves meanwhile in an irregular courtyard, filled with old copper water tanks, and surrounded by a medley of doors, arcades, and windows. One of the doors was open. Mrs. Schilizzi looked in, and discovered a miniature disused chapel, hanging on the very edge of the precipice. There was a book on the altar, some candlesticks, and some fragments of gold lace; and some fixed worm-eaten seats, which would have held perhaps twenty worshipers. The air seemed full to her of the prayers of dead generations, and suddenly she realized that in the seat nearest the altar, was a kneeling figure, habited in full armor, with its gauntleted hands clasped, and stretched toward the crucifix. Her insight told her, what she afterward discovered was the truth, that for hundreds of years had this figure remained there kneeling. Moved and awed, she hardly could tell why, she herself too sank on her knees, and half outstretched her hands in a similar rapt attitude. In a few minutes' time she rejoined Grenville outside. He saw that she wished to speak, but was afraid of her own voice. She found it at last, and taking hold of one of the buttons of his coat, she said, "Do you remember at the foot of the hill, we passed a poor woman, who was sitting with a sick baby? I want to go down, and see if we can't help her. I want to help someone—I want to do something good. Is this poetry—is this religion? What is happening to me? I hardly know myself."

He saw her swallow some strong access of agitation. He saw the effort undulate in her throat. "Wait," he said, "for a moment. Here is Fritz with the custodian. Fritz, at the foot of the castle, was a poor woman with a baby. Give her a florin; ask if she wants help; and tell her the lady will presently come and speak to her."

"She is here," said Fritz. "She is the custodian's wife. I think they are only tired. It is a long way to get up here."

The woman was entering the court at the very moment. Mrs. Schilizzi almost ran toward her; but moving gently as soon as she got near, spoke to her in a voice so gentle, that the woman looked up in wonder. Grenville saw her presently take the child in her arms, and carrying it, go with the mother through some low shadowy archway. The rose of her face presently came back again into the daylight. "I know," she said, "what it is that the child wants. I have told the woman it shall be sent to-morrow to her from Lichtenbourg."

They prepared now to follow the custodian through the building. While he was unlocking a door, she softly, as if forgetting herself, laid her hand upon Grenville's arm, and her cheek was near his shoulder. The rooms they entered were full of dust and echoes. They were bare of all furniture except a few dilapidated tables, and a multitude of rude portraits hanging on the whitewashed walls. But in place of furniture, in one room after another, were piles of rusty armor, heaped up like haystacks. They saw the quarters which the Baron was shortly to occupy, once the priest's, and almost as bare as the others. Saints and scenes from the Bible, almost obliterated by time, were daubed on the rough plaster; and if it had not been for some china pipes on racks, and some pairs of Hessian boots, they would still have seemed the abode of some ascetic of the Middle Ages. By and by descending a narrow staircase, they emerged through a low door, and found themselves in the open air again. They were on a narrow platform, hanging over the precipice; and all about them were loop-holed turrets and batterics, clinging to the rock like swallows' nests, and connected by scrambling stairs. The hush came over them, which is caused by the spectacle of a great depth. Presently they saw at one side of them a little triangular garden, supported on a ledge by parapets, and reached by some rough steps. There were a few bushes in it; and a bench on which they seated themselves. Looking toward the custodian they noticed that his head was bare. A second glance showed them he was standing under a wooden crucifix. There was in his face a hardy devout patience, and a manliness mixed with melancholy, that seemed strangely in keeping with the gaunt sacred image, embrowned by a thousand storms. They called him to them, and talked to him. He was grateful for their interest in his child, and showed a simple pleasure in telling them of his monotonous life. Once each week either he or his wife descended to the world below to purchase their scant necessaries; otherwise, they lived alone in this aerial solitude. Once a year a priest said mass in the chapel; once a year the baron came for a day or two; and now and then some visitors. These were his only incidents. They asked him to look for Fritz, and tell him to go on to the station and see that their dinner was ready for them, which they had ordered at the small restaurant.

The man went and left them alone together.

"You mustn't," she said presently, "take me to any more places like this."

"Why not?" he asked.

"I can't tell why it is," she said, "but they overwhelm me. If one's soul, if one's imagination, has a heart, as one's body has, they make mine throb and beat so that I can hardly live." She turned her eyes to him, sad like an evening sky. "I have lived," she said, "so seldom, or rather not at all. I am not accustomed to it." Presently she went on, "I don't know why I feel like this; but it's you, I think, who have set my imagination going. This rock, I suppose, is not tall enough to make it difficult for one's lungs to breathe; but as a rock of imagination it seems to touch the clouds; and here in the high silence the past is face to face with us. And yet," she said, pushing a stone with the tip of her parasol, "is it the past that moves me? I can't tell what it is. Look at the sunset. That too seems to be part of it."

"It is," said Grenville, "what I called romance or poetry, yesterday morning when we talked together at the mill. I see you understand it quite as well as I do—even better. I only stand on tiptoe—you float in the air."

"I wonder," she murmured, "if we have any right to float. Perhaps we were made only to walk—to plod."

"That," he said, "is a question we must each answer for ourselves. Fancy a stock broker trying to cultivate ecstasies, or St. Francis as a bull or bear. What is folly in most people is elevation in some. I tell you that for me this life I am now leading, is an episode only—a moment's return to his house of one of the younger sons of poetry, who has no inheritance in the ideal; and who must make his way, toiling among the furrows of prose."

As he said this, he was conscious that she flinched a little. "I suppose," she said, "all this elevation we talk of is a very fine thing for wise men to play with; but it is fit to fill the lives only of silly women. Your plaything may be our life; or if we find it is your plaything, our death."

"How quickly you misunderstand me," he said, "almost as quickly as you understand me. Listen and let me explain myself. You thought just now that I was laughing at you. I was afraid before, that you would be doing the same by me."

The tone of his voice reassured her. "Yes," she said, "explain. I am listening. How could you think I laughed at you?"

"If a man," he replied, "is too much of a dreamer, he easily becomes laughable; and my fear was not that you should think that I made a plaything of sentiments, of elevation, of poetry, or whatever we like to call it; but that I took it too seriously. Look—may I read you this? I was just on the point of showing it to you. It is a rough copy of something I meant to put in my diary. I scribbled it on the back of a letter when I was staying with the Princess. I begin by saying just what we said yesterday—that a love-marriage is an attempt to realize poetry in life; and then I go on like this: 'Such a love to which all life is subservient, is good for poets only, or for men whose career is imaginative art of some kind. There are others who can feel it, but who are no more than half poets, and who, if they succeed anywhere, must succeed in what is called the world. Now for such men love is the world's great rival, and the only match for the world at its own game. It is the ideal forever luring them away from the actual; and <u>filling life with a dream of impossible meaning</u>, it makes them hope for everything, and do nothing. During all my early life it had that effect on me; or rather, not it, but my belief in it, and my hope to find it. It is only since its power is broken that I am at last beginning to act; and I go on talking about it because I am so glad to be free from it; yes, and partly also because I sigh for its lost magic. And yet why should I sigh? I find I have no occasion.

I feared till very lately that my practical ambition had possibly taken root in me because my sense of life's poetry was dead, and that, if I gained the world, I should find I had paid my soul for it. But my experience in Hungary has shown me that my fear was false. Poetry, love, the ideal, has here come back to me, with all its old fascinations, but free from its old danger. The romance which I once sought to enjoy by personally enslaving myself to it, I enjoy now with the freedom of an artistic spectator; and I enjoy it all the more in life, because I am not troubled by it in my own life. Here is the difference between this romance and the other. I belonged to the other. This belongs to me."

"How foolish," she said, "I must seem to you. You must be forbearing with me, because I have shown you my weakness. Your career is not art; but you take all this as an artist. To me it is nothing at all; or else it is life— it is religion."

"You know," he replied, after a pause, "that space has three dimensions. So has life; and as lived by different people it may consist of different movements—of lateral movements, or a movement upward. The movement upward is the movement of saints, and poets, and yourself. The reason is that they and that you have wings. I have long lost mine; they fell from me with my boy's curls. And yet when you talk to me I feel the fanning of yours."

She rose from her seat, and looked down at him.

"Do you know what you do?" she said. "It is something that you shouldn't. Instead of saying what is true, you say the thing which is the very exact opposite. Look at your watch, will you; for I think, to judge by the light, that instead of a movement upward, we ought to begin one downward."

As they went together down the winding road, unnoticed by him she often turned and looked at him with the curious intentness of a child.

Suddenly she said, laughing, "Had you curls, when you were a little boy?"

He laughed too, and again admitted that he had.

"When you were a little boy," she asked, "what name did they call you?"

He told her it was "Bobby."

She repeated the word softly. "That," she said, "was my brother's name." She looked him in the face for a moment, and once more repeated "Bobby."

"And you," he said, laughing, "when you were a little girl, I know what they called you; for your name no one would alter. It was Irma—Miss Irma—little Irma."

CHAPTER XI.

THAT evening, before she went to bed, inspired by the events of the day she produced the sheets of her diary; and having given her children's eyelids the gentle benediction of her kiss, she drew a long sigh, and began writing as follows:

"I have had during the last two days, an entirely new experience. I have met a man who cares to talk to me, because he understands my thoughts; and who does not look at me with the eyes of a cowardly beast of prey. At first he did not care to look at me at all. Well—even that, though it humbled me, is better than the ways of other men, though at times, for despised moments these have flattered my vanity. At first, too, I thought he laughed at me. Perhaps he did. As a member of society he thought nothing of me; and I have no doubt thinks nothing now. I am glad; for somehow, in that case, I am more touched by the change in him. Except once —and then it seemed unnatural to him—so far as I can remember, he has never paid me a compliment, unless it be the compliment of understanding me; and he talks to me not about myself, but about the things that are more than myself to me. To be understood! to me the very thought is astonishment. The sensation is so strange to me it makes me a new creature. I think it is Carlyle, or some German quoted by Carlyle, who says that a thought gains infinitely in value to the thinker, when he finds that another shares it. The same is the case with feeling. Bobby—I mean Bobby my brother—described once to me the pleasure he felt in China, at hearing in some strange place, the sound of his own language. For the first time in my life I have heard someone talk mine. He does more. He not only talks my language but enlarges it; for in addition to saying things that I have often said before, he says others that I have never said, but which become mine the moment he has said them. Naturally he only knows a part of me; but what he does know, he knows better than I myself do. He seems to have liberated in me a host of thoughts that were in prison.

"How freely I am writing. That I can do so, is all to his credit; for it is a witness to the fact that he has never tried to make love to me. He has the manner of a man who has made love to others; but he certainly has not done so to me. It would have been easy for him to do so, considering the subjects we talked about; but I noticed this—that whenever love was mentioned, he carefully divested his voice of any note of sentiment, and contrived to give me the same secure unembarrassed feeling I should have had if we were talking politics. What have I written? much more unembarrassed than that. I know nothing of politics, and couldn't talk about them if I tried.

"And yet, on certain grounds, I do not feel so secure. To be understood in this way spoils me. It is taking me away from the hard benches and the starved table of a school, to which I must return; and is showing me what my life might be—a thing which I had best forget. He said that poets made a spring in the world's mind, calling out sleeping flowers. His understanding me has done the same in mine. Little phrases of his stick in my mind; and wherever one of them rests a flower has blossomed. I express what has happened to me by such an odd succession of metaphors. I feel as if I were floating—as if I were being taken off my feet. He—no, not he, but the fact that he has understood me—makes my thoughts rise like a kite on wind."

Next day she continued thus:

"We are going to-morrow to see Count T——'s hotel in the forest. Mr. Grenville came in after the children's dinner to arrange about it; and an incident happened which confirms me in all I thought about him. It was simple in itself, and yet I hardly know how to write it; for in a certain sense it touches myself so closely. I will try, however, and see how the words come. The waiter, in laying the table, had moved some of my books—a pile of them; and had put them on a chair near the window. Many of them were English poets. Mr. Grenville took some of them up, and made some remark about the library I carried about with me. I thought of telling him—but I had not the courage to do so—that I was making some notes about English poets, and the kind of feeling they had felt and expressed for Nature. I did say that I was making some notes; and he smiled and appeared interested, saying, I see you have underlined a lot of Wordsworth.' And then all of a sudden, under the books of poetry, he came on a heap of horrible French novels. I call them horrible: but, as I have said before, they were classics; they were not books that it need be necessarily a disgrace to read; but the moment he noticed them, I saw him give a look at me, and his voice and his expression changed. 'Your tastes are catholic,' he said, as he took one of them up. 'They're not,' I exclaimed, 'if you mean I've a taste for those. I didn't know they were here. They were packed up by mistake. I never knew I had them till this morning. Take them away—do. I have been always meaning to burn them.' I spoke with so much sincerity, that he at once became all right again. His face had a look of relief which said plainly 'I misjudged her.' But I still felt shy and awkward, and hurried on to explain myself. I said what a pity it was that books so full of genius, should have so much in them that one wished to forget having even so much as looked at. 'I know,' I said, 'one is always told that they are justified because they are true; and perhaps they are true, and so novels ought to be: but the impression they leave on one is, not that they are true, but that they are bad.'

"Now how I arrived at the conclusion I don't know, except that it was by instinct; but I am as certain, as if he had said in so many words, that he thought these books bad books for me personally. And he was right; they have been bad. But without dropping the subject he managed to give it a turn, which seemed to completely separate it from any connection with myself. 'These books,' he said, 'though, like you, I admire their genius, and also their truth, as compared with novels meant for the schoolroom, really *are* bad for some people; but for people like you and me, I believe the bad, the offensive, quality in them, is artistic badness rather than moral badness. I believe that in novels written for grown-up people, all sides of life should be treated with equal fairness; but the human imagination is so constituted that six lines written about certain matters, will impress us with their reality quite as distinctly as six pages written about others. The French school of novelists, such as we now are talking of, wholly forget this; and though they may not give more space to the sensual side of man than to the mental, they produce on the mind of the reader a far more vivid impression of it. That is the artistic badness. The moral badness is this—that the impression with weak readers, corrupts the judgment long before it has appealed to it. And the novels we speak of are morally and artistically bad—not because they represent passion, but because they excite passion.'

"How true this is! I feel to myself to be so true that I could hardly have imagined it possible to discuss it with a man thus plainly; but there was something, not only in his phrases and in his way of putting the case, but in his tone and his manner also—something so full of a delicate and chivalrous feeling for me, that I had no sense of embarrassment. I was conscious of two things only—of being profoundly interested and also profoundly touched.

"He took the books with him. May I never see them again—them, nor any like them!

"I was just preparing to put my papers away when this happened. On the table I write stands a little oval looking-glass in a Dresden china frame. I happened to look in it, quite by accident, and noticed my own reflection. I am not vain—but I must confess this—I saw I was looking charming. Mr. Grenville, I believe, doesn't think me a bit pretty. Most men have thought nothing else about me. I am glad Mr. Grenville is like that. I like him to see in me the good points I am in doubt about; not those about which I am certain. And yet, being a woman, I must in truth admit that I should like him to realize I was pretty, just as a fact of nature. I've a good mind, out of curiosity, to ask him if he does do so.

"To-morrow—yes, to-morrow, we are going into the heart of the forest. These expeditions to me are like her first balls to a girl. Everything is so unaccountably, so unfathomably fresh to me."

Before composing herself to sleep she knelt up in her bed, her hands crossed on the folds of her white drapery. She did not, even mentally, say any definite word, for the influences to which, as she grew up, her religion had been subjected, hardly admitted of this; but she let her soul like a sunflower turn to something beyond her and above her, as she rested for some moments in the attitude of an infant Samuel. When she closed her eyes now there was no frown on her forehead, but a placid faith in the day toward which sleep would waft her.

Faith in this case was certainly not disappointed. A light varnished carriage, whose brownness shone in the morning, adapted for rough roads, and drawn by four active little horses, who jingled bells as they moved and tossed red tassels, took them away with a speed that was in itself exhilaration. Out of the town they sped, through valleys and fields and orchards. Then came ground that was wilder, plantations of pine, and spaces covered with pine needles. Rocks cropped up through the soil, and prickly bushes dotted it. At last they entered a great undulating forest, where the branches whispered and the breath of the pine trees floated. Through this they drove for a good two hours at least, encountering all the way hardly a sign of life except some men who, in one place, were busy mending the road, and a wagon which they overtook, laden with chairs and tables, and which, as they surmised, must be bound for the Count's hotel.

They had arranged to picnic in the hunting lodge, and go to the hotel from thence. A sloping expanse, covered with heath and bog myrtle, at last appeared, like an island in the sea of foliage. Driving up this, and passing through a belt of trees, they saw the lodge before them—a whitewashed building, with a high-pitched tiled roof, and an open arcade by which the few rooms were connected. Fritz soon produced the forester and his wife, who took charge of it; and having made them aware who his master was, it was hardly a minute before the principal doors were open, and their hamper of provisions was being carried into the principal sitting-room.

Mrs. Schilizzi was in the happiest mood possible, and Grenville had caught it from her, in all its buoyant freshness. They insisted on being left to unpack their hamper for themselves; and she exclaimed with delight at the various delicacies contained in it, taxing him laughingly with being wrong and extravagant in having ordered them. Every unfolded package had all the savor of a discovery; every missing requisite, which they asked the old woman to supply, was the occasion of an adventure. Grenville ran her to earth in her own kitchen regions, and came back with stories of her pots and pans and her cooking stove, and she presently followed him in with a pile of plates and some old Bohemian glasses, with coats-of-arms in color on them. While she was arranging them and putting the last touches to the table, Grenville and Mrs. Schilizzi took stock of the room—its bare polished floor, its velvet chairs and sofas, stiffly grouped together at one end round a table; they peeped into a writing-room, and a charming bedroom beyond; they examined some pieces of tapestry and a large number of horns, which formed the only decorations of the rudely distempered walls; and then at last they looked out of the windows. They turned to each other with delight, for straight before them, at a distance of a hundred yards or so, was the smooth glass of a lake, full of the sky and pine woods, which stretched itself out to a breadth of several miles, and reached away curving into some indefinite distance.

The pleasure of this prospect added a new zest to their meal. Its microscopic incidents were sufficient to fill the moment—the pouring out of the wine, the cutting up of the chicken, the extracting the salt from the paper packets that held it. They experienced together that most charming form of confidence—the common unashamed enjoyment of little things such as these. No thought seemed too small to communicate, no sense of amusement too trifling to share. Then they went out to inspect the landscape in the neighborhood, having first asked the way to the Count's hotel. The way, they presently found, hardly required asking; for the building was full in sight, at about a furlong's distance. It stood near to the lake, and was somewhat Swiss in appearance, surrounded with wooden balconies, and shaded by projecting roofs. They entered. It was full of a smell of newly planed wood and varnish. Though it was not yet open, the furnishing was nearly complete, and the manager was beside himself with delight at showing his accommodation to the strangers. Some private suites were already fit for occupation; nothing was wanting but some fittings for the public salons. "The air," said the manager, "owing to the nearness of the pine trees, is supposed to be healthier even than that of Lichtenbourg, and the neighboring mineral spring has properties quite unique. Will not your excellencies honor me by taking coffee?"

They told him that the woman at the lodge was at that moment preparing some; and they slowly strolled back enchanted with all about them. There were grassy slopes, tufted with aromatic shrubs; there were glimpses of cart tracks leading away into the forest; there were reeds by the lakeside up to their waists in water; and a beech tree in front of the lodge made a shade on the warm soil. Here they had their coffee; their tray rested on the beech husks, and they themselves lay on some rugs beside it. During luncheon everything had reminded her of something in her childhood—of picnics with her brothers and sisters, and of absurd shifts they were put to. She told him how Dick stole her pocket-handkerchief for a napkin, and how Olga and Daisy used to say, "Do look at Irma gobbling." And Grenville had thought, though he forbore to tell her so, that he saw that submerged childhood shining still at the bottom of her eyes. Now, however, her mood had become more pensive. She talked not of the amusements of her childhood, but of its charms and dreams. "There were reeds like those," she said, "in a lake that was near our home. I used often to sit by them and wonder how Pan could have made his pipes." Then gradually one thing after another recalled to her her father's garden, its tall trees and its flower beds. Each memory as it floated into her mind shaped itself into artless words; and now and then she would call Grenville's attention to something in the scene before her—some ripple of sunlight on the lake, or the ruddy or silvery bark of some gleaming tree, which appealed to her for its own sake only.

This quality in her of sensitiveness to natural beauty, struck Grenville afresh; and as they were driving back he kept thinking it over, and at last gave his thoughts utterance. She again told him, as she had told him once before, "that his appreciations were far deeper than hers."

"I think," he said, "they are just the same appreciations, only mine are like pictures in oil, on a canvas already painted on; yours are in transparent colors, shining on fresh white paper. Mine are like dusty, yours are like dewy, leaves; but when I see things with you, the feeling I have is this—that the dew on your thoughts sprinkles the dust on mine."

Later on, as the sun was beginning to set, and the lower tracts of the sky were flushing between the feathery branches, he said to her, "I have often wondered, noticing how mere colors of scenes like these move your sense of beauty, and stir your imagination—I have often wondered how you would be moved and stirred by Italy —by the sea, the skies, and the hills, as they shine through the crystal air."

"Ah!" she exclaimed softly, "if I could only see them!"

"I have seen them often," he continued, "but I have always seen them alone—I mean alone as regards any real enjoyment of them. If I have been looking at anything that has specially moved me—whose witchery, as your friend Wordsworth says, has melted into my heart—I have never had anyone with me able to feel the same, or with whom I could exchange even a broken exclamation of pleasure. You, I think, would be pleased with just the same things as I am. All sorts of scenes and objects and aspects of things come floating into my mind at this moment, which I am sure would make you hold your breath by their beauty."

"Tell me," she said, "what sort of things."

He answered her slowly, as if he were talking to himself, enumerating chance memories. "The marble peaks," he began, "of the pure Carrara mountains, rising out of violent mist, and glittering in a sky of primrose color—the turquoise-colored crescent of water which one sees framed in the ilexes, under whose shade Shelley wrote "The Cenci"—white sands I have walked by in the hush of the morning, while the dark blue waters slept on them—boats gliding on Como with sails like the breasts of swans. I should like to be with you when you were looking at things like these—when you were listening to the songs of the peasants floating at dusk among the fire-flies, or the notes of the angelus trembling, some near, some distant, from half a dozen craggy villages among the Apennines."

"That is enough," she said. "Let me think a little of that. Every word is a picture; I wish we could see it all." Then suddenly she turned to him, and, looking at him with a smile of curiosity, "But you told me," she said, "that Italy was a place that represented prose to you."

She heard him sigh faintly, and for a moment he did

not speak. "I remember," he said at last. "But that was only on a special occasion; and it was due to—how shall we put it? to extraneous, or (shall we say?) adventitious, circumstances."

"What grand words!" she laughed. "I wonder what the circumstances were."

"I am not sure whether, supposing you care to hear, I may not one day tell you. If ever I do, you will know something about me, which at the present moment I hardly know myself."

When they reached Lichtenbourg it was latish. She was tired, and dined in her room. Grenville said to himself, among the clatter of plates in the restaurant, "It seems as if a brook had been rippling at my side all day, and the god Pan or somebody had filled all the reeds with music."

As for her, she was really thoroughly tired. She felt the truth of what she had said to him at parting, when he had asked whether she were inclined to dine with him. "One must not crowd too much into a single day." She glanced at her diary, and pushed it wearily away from her; but then with a change of purpose, for a moment or two she sat down before it, and hastily wrote on the page the following lines from Tennyson, with some blots, above and below it, meant to do duty for asterisks:

> Across the hills and far away,
>   Beyond their utmost purple rim,
> And deep into the dying day
>   The happy princess followed him.

CHAPTER XII.

THEY had made no plans for the following day, but he took it for granted that he should spend it with her somewhere and somehow; and he was pleased rather than surprised when, before ten o'clock, a note was brought to him from her, begging him to come to her instantly. He was surprised, however, as soon as he was in her presence; for her face and manner were full of trouble and agitation. "I have just," she said, "heard such dreadful news; and I can't at all tell what's the best thing to be done. The doctor—a very nice man, who has seen the children before—has just told me that scarlatina has broken out in Lichtenbourg—that three children have already died of it, and that there are two bad cases in the villa next the hotel. I want," she went on, "to be off without a moment's unnecessary delay; but I am so perplexed—I can't decide where to go. I might return to my aunt; but the children are never well at the castle; and of course we have our flat at Vienna; but Vienna, in this heat, would be death to them. Poor little things—they are both of them so delicate! And then," she added with a faint regretful laugh, "everything here was beginning to be so pleasant. Do help me—tell me what you advise."

Grenville's face while she was speaking, had shown as much concern as her own; but by the time she had ended, its expression had changed suddenly, and he looked at her for a moment in silence, with a dawning smile.

"Can't you help me?" she said a little irritably. "To me this is really serious. I, whatever you may do, see in it nothing to smile at."

"I was smiling," he said, "at something you don't see; and that is a way, and an easy one, out of all your difficulties. Take your children to the Count's hotel in the forest."

The suggestion came to her like a burst of sunshine out of clouds. She drew her breath and clasped her hands with delight at it. But then, relapsing into despondency, she sighed, "The hotel's not open."

"No," urged Grenville, "but some of the rooms are ready; and we know the cook's there. No doubt they could take you in. If you'll let me, I'll order a horse, and ride over to arrange about it; and you meanwhile can take the opinion of the doctor."

She paused reflecting; then she looked at him inquiringly. "And what would you do?" she said. "Would you stay here? You couldn't—at least I suppose so—you couldn't very well come to the hotel."

"I," he said, "would go to the Count's hunting lodge. As I told you the other day, it is already as good as lent to me."

"It's too good of you," she murmured. "But how bored you would be shut up there!"

"As soon as I am," he answered, "I promise you I will go away. Only tell me—shall I ride over now and arrange things?"

"Yes; do what you can; and I shall be waiting for

your report anxiously. Don't be too long—not longer than you can help."

This parting injunction kept softly echoing in his ears, as his horse's hoofs rang on the road of yesterday; and he was back again, his mission accomplished before she had begun expecting him. The manager, he said, had been charmed at his prompt return, and more charmed still on finding out the reason of it. A suite of rooms with a lovely view of the lake, were perfectly ready at this moment for occupation; and though as yet there were only a few servants, there were still sufficient to wait upon one family. As for himself, Grenville had been at the lodge. The forester and his wife had heard from the Count that morning, that the English Excellency was to occupy it whenever it pleased him; and "By this time," he said, "they will be airing the sheets and dusting. If we go to-morrow afternoon we shall find everything prepared for us; and in case at the hotel there should be difficulty the first night about dinner, I have ordered something at six, for ourselves and for the children, at the lodge."

"I see," she said laughing, "you will have everything your own way; and as the doctor approves of the plan, we are all bound to be grateful to you. You must, too, arrange about the carriages. Our flight will be a regular exodus."

And indeed with the luggage and the servants, and the children, it seemed so. It was a journey slower than their first, and so far as scenery went, it could not offer them the excitement and charm of novelty; but they felt in it a novelty of some kind—they hardly could tell what; and though the place to which it was taking them was still fresh in their memories, the life to which it was taking them had something in it that was hardly imaginable.

Columbus, when he landed first in the New World, could not have felt in his nerves the thrill of entire strangeness more keenly than they did, when they finally reached their destination. The halt of the three carriages at the wooden porch of the hotel, the bustle of the servants, the sorting of the luggage, the taking of hers indoors, and the dispatch of his to the lodge, seemed to them both like events that never had had a parallel. They inspected her rooms together, and admired their fresh daintiness; they went out on the balcony, and admired the lake and forest. The children were wild with delight, as if they had never before been happy; and the mother clapped her hands and laughed as happily as the children.

Then Grenville hurried off to the lodge, promising to return and bring them over to dinner. The gold of the warm evening shone and floated on the lake, when he did so an hour later, and when they went with him across the grass and the pine needles—the children in their red frocks, and their mother, with apologies to Grenville, showing the woodlands the cloak in which she had glittered at Lichtenbourg. The meal which they found awaiting them was a supper rather than dinner. There was fish from the lake, a chicken, and a variety of early vegetables. There was for the elders a slim bottle of hock, and an old German jug full of milk for the children. The mellow daylight was still bright enough for them to eat by; but some candles were burning, whose flames were like pale daffodils.

"When we were little," Mrs. Schilizzi said, "we had a game which we called 'pretending.' One could play it in many ways; but our favorite way was this. We put a tent we had on the back of an old donkey, and we walked away to a common at the back of the house. We pitched our tent, we encamped among the furze bushes, we lit a fire, and pretended we were Arabs in the desert. Those encampments have always seemed to me the remotest places in the world, and the hours we spent there the most adventurous life imaginable. I feel somehow as if we were playing at 'pretending' now." She said this when the meal was drawing to a close; and then she added presently, laughing into her children's eyes, "Now, children, there is another adventure in store for you. You must come back with mother a long, long way to bed, all across the grass and through the myrtle bushes, where the beautiful fairies play."

The children opened their eyes, and they were deep with the joys of imagination.

"Must we go yet?" said Grenville. "Won't you wait for our coffee?"

"No," she answered, laying her hand on his arm. "They are tired; it is very late for them. Get them their hats, and let us go. We will come back for our coffee."

As they went in the dusk, the children played among the bushes, constantly running up to their elders to ask where were the fairies; and Mrs. Schilizzi said, "Whenever a child sees them, they become shy and change themselves into glow-worms."

She and Grenville, when they went back to the lodge, drank their coffee by the window in almost complete silence. Now and then one or other of them uttered a word or two; he offered her a biscuit; he asked her if she felt the draught; and once, unbidden, he rose and bent down over her, and folded her cloak a little more closely round her.

"Won't you smoke?" she said. "You look so natural when you are doing so."

By and by, between the floating puffs of his cigarette, he said abruptly, "We must know each other very well, I think."

She asked why? as if sure of the answer and yet waiting for it.

"Because we can sit like this," he said, "and talk without ever speaking."

For a time she made no response, except a look and a faint smile. But at last she rose from her seat, and said, "It is time to go." He expostulated, telling her it was early; and indeed it was only nine.

"Don't keep me," she said very softly and gently. "Let me go. If you like you can walk back with me."

They were both standing by this time, but both seemed withheld from moving. Suddenly she uttered a word, quite naturally, and as if she hardly knew she was using it; but it went through his whole being as if it had been a spell. It was simply his own name, "Bobby." He waited. Her head drooped pensively.

"There is something," she went on slowly, "that I want to tell you. You have been very good to me—you have taken great care of me."

Again she stopped. "This is all so new," she murmured. "It is like— No, I don't know what it's like. It's like nothing except itself—to me." Then, with a sudden movement, she raised her head, came up to him, and put her hands on his coat. In the frank appeal of her eyes, in every look and gesture there was an absolute simplicity, as if her inmost self were expressing itself.

"Bobby," she said, lingering over the syllable in a whisper, "I want you to be always good to me—always. Tell me that you will be; tell me in my ear that you will be."

Her words seemed like the bleat of some forsaken animal. A silence followed, and only her eyes spoke. There was a trouble in them like the meeting of two conflicting waters. A moment later she had hidden her face in her hands, and when she removed them, in her eyes there were tears and happiness. He had uttered her as yet no word; but now looking half sadly at her, "Irma," he said, "I will be to you the best I am able to be. You are right, you must go now. Come, I will take you back."

If her day's journey had tired her, it had, at all events, not made her sleepy. A lamp stood on her table; her window was half open; a faint sound as of murmuring boughs came in through it; and before her, according to her custom, was the case that contained her diary. The last words she had written were the lines she took from Tennyson. "Unity of style as a diarist was not her strong point certainly;" nor did what she wrote now show any concern to make it so. It was hardly like a diary, indeed, except that it was prefaced by a date.

"To-night," she began, "if I am to express myself at all, I must express myself in a new way. I must address myself to something that is not myself, and that is beyond me. What this is I cannot tell, or, at all events,

I will not tell. I will not tell myself even. Its form and its nature shall remain vague, and I shall speak to it more freely. Listen then, you, whatever you are, to whom I am going to lay bare my thoughts, as the sea lays bare to the moon its hushed and yet troubled waves. I used when a child to read Ovid's "Metamorphosis," and I often amused myself by wondering how the people felt when they found themselves turning into trees and flowers and fountains. I think I can tell now, for I am undergoing the same sort of change myself.

"Power to whom I speak, into what am I changing? You will be able to see perhaps; but I want myself to tell you. Could I laugh about it—and why should I not? for one can always afford to laugh when one is quite sure one is serious—I would tell you that I felt like Aaron's rod, when it budded. As for Ovid, the bodies of his women turned into flowers. I feel like a flower turning into a woman's soul. Is not this vague? Tell me—can you catch my meaning? I wish to put it more plainly; and when I try to do so in my mind, do you know what happens? The sentences I shape to myself are metamorphosed like Ovid's heroines; and instead of speaking about myself, I find myself speaking about— what? About the warm silence of the night, about the stealing scents of the forest, that just make the edge of the thin lace curtains tremble, about the lapping of the lake, that I can just hear at intervals, as at intervals when one is half asleep, one can just hear one's watch tick. Yes, I feel inclined to tell you about all these things, instead of telling you—of confessing to you, about myself. But were I really talking to you, and could you hear my voice, I should betray myself in that;

you would hear my whole confession in it. Consider again. Is this a sign of anything? I write these sentences slowly, pausing between each and dreaming—dreaming as I watch the flames of the candles tremble, and little white drops of wax chase one another down their sides; and as I dream, with my pen balanced in my hand, all sorts of verses I have read come, like bees in summer, winging their way into my mind; and each comes laden with some new meaning, all my own—some pollen, some honey, some dew, out of the flower of life, as I myself have lived it.

"Can you imagine how a rose feels, when all its petals are unfolding? That is how I feel. I am unfolding toward you. Do you see what you have done for me? Ah, but that is not all the story. If you have done this for me, there is something I have done for you. Let me boast—let me rise in the air, on this sense of power. You—you who are so much stronger than I am, I have led you, I have influenced you: and listen; you know I have done this—I have opened your eyes, and you have seen in me what I never saw, but only dreamed of in myself, till you saw it; and now I am created anew. Since you have seen it, it is a reality.

"Shall I go further—shall I make another boast? If you would ever see what I am writing, I would not; but you never will, and so I will make it. Something—I know what it was: it was regard for me, for I saw that in your eyes—well, something has held you back from me, or held you up from me. I thought all the more of you for this; but I have made you stoop; my power has been more than yours. I have made you stoop till your lips have at last touched mine. And do you know how I did it? I will remind you. I begged you—not in so many words, but you knew my meaning—I begged you, I prayed you, to keep away from me. And I meant it too. I have never lied to you. But there was something in me that meant something quite different, and meant it more strongly—at least I suppose so; for we now see the result. Perhaps I shall teach you what a strange thing a woman's heart is. Its motto, I think, ought to be, 'I am nothing if logical.'

"And yet, seeing that in all this some responsibility has been incurred somewhere, I don't mean to let you off, and say you are responsible for nothing. For do you know what you have done? I wonder, I wonder, if you do? You have entered my mind, you have moved among my thoughts, like a wind moving through a garden, and stealing into the flowers, and fluttering their petals. You have been where no human being has ever been before—not even I myself; and you have said to me, 'See these flower beds, see these flowers. You never knew, did you, that you had such things in your garden?' Why did you do this? You had no business to come there and wander there at all. But since you have come, do you know how I am going to punish you? I am going to keep you there. You never shall go away again.

"I began talking of you vaguely, as some impersonal power, and owing to a kind of shyness I thought of you vaguely; but by this time I think I have pretty well betrayed myself. And yet I can no more tell you now, than I could at the beginning, all that I want to tell you. Let the air of the night, which we both are breathing, breathe it to you; let the forest murmur it. Let the lake, which is so near you, ripple it to you through your windows. Let me tell it to you myself, in telling you how I love my children. I feel sometimes as if nothing I could do for them, could ever satisfy what I feel for them; that they could never be close enough to my heart; that my life could never completely enough be spent for theirs. As the arms of a mother long to enfold her child, so, my friend, my companion, I long to enfold you!"

The following morning when she stepped out on her balcony, while a waiter inside was clattering as he arranged the children's breakfast, she murmured, feeling the freshness that seemed to pervade everything, "And the evening and the morning were the first day."

She presently looked toward the lodge, watching the slope in front of it; but she saw no one stirring; and a shadow—a very transparent shadow—of disappointment crossed her mind. "Does he like me," she said to herself, as she passed indoors. But the smile on her lips showed that she had little doubt about the answer.

At breakfast a packet was brought to her.

"What!" she exclaimed. "The post! I never thought that letters would follow me here so soon." But she saw, the next moment, that it was something which had come by hand; and she found, on undoing it, that it was a copy of Grenville's poems. She recollected now that she had asked him if he had a copy which he could lend her. He had said, "No"; but a line which he now inclosed ran thus: "By accident this was found in one of my boxes. I will come to you after breakfast. You have made me once more a poet." She turned over the pages with a placid, half-tender, interest; but all of a sudden she started and blushed crimson. She had come to the fly leaf; and that showed her his meaning, when he spoke of being once more a poet. Her initials were written on it; and under her initials these lines:

> What may I write that shall hint of my love for you?
> My pen trembles idly, and doubts as it dips.
> Teach me some name that is tender enough for you:
> Or else hold me silent, my love, with your lips.

She read the lines over and over again, her lips slightly quivering. Then, pressing her hands, with the open book in them, close to her breast, as if feeling some sharp pain, but a pain contradicted by something shining in her eyes, "Oh, my friend," she murmured, "my beloved friend—speech is silver."

CHAPTER XIII.

MRS. SCHILIZZI remained for some time, with the book lying open in her lap, and her eyes fixed on the verses as if they were some strange flower. She had left the breakfast-table, and was sitting outside on the balcony, shielding her head from the sun with a large parasol, while a light breeze played with the soft tendrils of her hair. Her parasol and her dress were red; and as Grenville came presently over to the hotel from the hunting lodge, he saw her from far off, like one brilliant patch of color. She, however, did not see him, till he came to her through the window of the sitting-room, and the sounds of his steps roused her. She gave him her good-morning, except with her eyes. She looked up at him, her hand still resting on the book; and she merely said "How could you?" He returned her gaze, not with sadness exactly, but with gravity; and for a few moments both were silent. At last he said, "Are you angry with what I write? It was written before I knew what I was writing."

"No," she said, "not with it, but with myself for being made so happy by it."

Again they were both silent. At length, in an altered voice, "Tell me," he said, "what shall we do this morning? The manager tells me that he has a pony carriage, and also that there are roads in the forest—a little rough, but still fit for driving."

"Oh," she exclaimed, "let us drive!" And her face was like a sunlit sea from which the shadow of a summer cloud had floated. The carriage was ordered, and they drove off together, first for a little way skirting the borders of the lake, and then following the road, into the heart of the leaves and shadow. Active glancing lights were playing on all sides among the branches; birds sang, squirrels whisked their tails; and the white throat of a stoat confronted them, tame with wonder. Mrs. Schilizzi seemed to Grenville, as she sat beside him, to bear the same relation to the beauty and the happiness of nature, that an echo bears to a voice; and she filled his mental ear with a soft magical music. Every appreciation he shared with her, every passing laugh, was a new link uniting him to her, that was fashioned and fastened noiselessly.

Having driven for some way among pines, they at last reached a wood of beeches, where the undergrowth was cut into glades, evidently for the purposes of sport, and where the open ground was gleaming with moss and grasses. They left the pony in charge of a boy they had taken with them, and wandered away together through one of these inviting ways. By and by they seated themselves at the foot of a tree, she more flower-like than ever, in her red dress among the greenness, while her cheeks seemed, by contrast, like the petals of a pale geranium.

"Never," wrote Grenville afterward, addressing her in imagination, "never shall I forget that scene. After we had sat there for a moment or two, talking of I cannot remember what, you turned to me with a half mischievous laugh, and yet with something in your manner that was serious, and you said to me, 'Bobby'—you said that slowly, as if you liked the word—'I should think you were a brother, if it were not for one thing; and that is, that I want to ask you a such a silly and vain question. Do you think I am pretty?' Irma, there was nothing of the coquette in you. You asked that question with such absolute simplicity, laughing at yourself just a little for asking it, that you made me absolutely simple in my answer. I said, 'I should, very likely, think so, if only you were anybody but yourself. As it is, I see not your face, but the meaning of it. Many hieroglyphics are very graceful in form, and so long as they are nothing but forms for us we, no doubt, think them pretty; but as soon as we learn to read them, we forget the prettiness of the letters, in thinking of the sense of the sentences.' And yet you were pretty, and I saw you were. Round your red dress through the mosses, blue flowers were sprouting, like tiny spires; and above you the young leaves of the beech trees were catching the sunlight on their tremulous transparent films; and we had for companions the hush and whisper of the forest, and the profound embowered solitude. . . . .

"Irma, you turned over in your mind what I said to you, as if you were a little girl sucking a sugar plum, and thinking whether you liked it; and at last I saw that you did like it, and you said, 'I'm glad of that. I hate people who like me merely because I am pretty.' We were both satisfied; and for a little while we did nothing but pull up grasses and flowers, and ask each other if we knew their names. We are neither of us very good at botany. Presently you began to tell me of a place in a wood near your old home, where you used to go and hide yourself with your books. There was a copy of Keats you used to take with you, and an 'As you Like It': and on one of them, I forget which, you had managed to spill some milk, and your brothers and sisters used to say of you, 'Irma is always so messy.' And you laughed as you told me this, and said, 'I am very clean now.' And then you began telling me one little anecdote after another about your early years, and all the atmosphere of your life's spring breathed about me. You seemed to be bringing out all your little treasures, and showing them to me one by one, with a child's simplicity mixed with a woman's humor; and with something more than this—with consciousness that to me you would never have thought of showing them, if you had not been confident that whatever was yours would interest me. There lay the magic of the moment, its subtle spiritual alchemy, transmuting so much within me.

"What trifles such things are! Any man not a fool can in some moods laugh at them; a fool can laugh at them in all moods indiscriminately; but no man not a fool will be afraid of his own laughter. Men who know life best, and whose sense of humor is keenest, know best that we should never find anything to be valuable if we valued only what we could never despise or laugh at. The serious things of life are of value only as settings for the things which in our practical moods we call trifles. Let me think of ourselves in that wood, and compare ourselves with some man of business, who has made at one stroke by his shrewdness some twenty thousand pounds. *There* is sense—*there* is seriousness, with a vengeance. Well, what does this good man do with his money? He buys for his wife some magnificent tiara of diamonds.

But what are these diamonds? Merely sparkling pebbles. Consider this: the reward of business is to look at some little pebbles twinkling. This is the pleasure of your shrewd practical man. What is that compared with my vision of you?

"Well, after you had talked to me of those enchanted trifles, you suddenly checked yourself, and you said to me, 'Look here, I am doing all the talking. I tell you everything, and you tell me nothing. It's your turn now. You must tell things to me.' I asked you what sort of things. You reflected a little; and then looking at me, Irma, with a persuasive gravity, you said, 'Tell me why Italy seemed a prosaic place to you.' I hesitated, for reasons which you know now. They concerned another woman; and the devotion and respect I felt for you, and my sense of how impossible it would be for me, under any circumstances, to discuss you with anyone else, gave me the same reverential feeling with regard to the woman I speak of. There seemed to be something wanting to justify me in even naming her. And yet I spoke the truth when I answered you, 'I should like to tell you, but it would take a long time.' And here, having mentioned time, I found an escape out of my difficulty. I pulled out my watch, and showed you how late it was. You started and laughed. 'Help me up,' you said; and as quick as our feet could carry us, we went to the pony carriage and returned. I lunched with you at the hotel. How well I remember the look of that meal. The brown crumpled skin of the children's rice pudding, and the clear blue shadows the dishes made on the table-cloth! I remember, too, saying, as we entered the room together, 'So far as liking goes, I should like to tell you everything.'

"That evening, Irma, that evening, I did so.

"In the afternoon you had letters to write; so had I. You wrote yours in a summer house by the lake, with your children playing round you. I went to write mine in my own rooms. But write I could not. I could not concentrate my thoughts on the people I wanted to address, or the subjects I wanted to deal with. Between me and the paper your image would come; and five minutes after five minutes I found myself sitting motionless, occupied with it only. At last I gave the attempt up, and pushed my pen away from me. I longed to go back to you; but I thought it the kindest thing to give you one hour to yourself at all events; so I kept myself from you for all that weary time. I never knew before how long an hour could be, or how in an hour a sense of want could be developed in one, springing up like a tree that grows under the napkin of an Indian juggler. At the end of that hour I went to you, and found you still in the summer house. 'Have you written your letters?' I asked. You pointed to two sheets of note paper, on each of which were scribbled a few lines, and which you began listlessly to put into their envelopes. 'I couldn't write,' you said. 'That is all I have done.' Irma, that pleased me. We had been going through the same experience. But when you said you were tired, and wanted to lie down for an hour in your room. 'Do you mind?' you asked me. Of course I said no; but owing to one of those wayward caprices of temper, which sometimes take the bit of reason in their mouths, and carry off the imagination on their backs, I said to myself that you were tired because you were tired of me. Well—you went; and for another hour I was left alone. Fool that I was! I felt miserable, despised, deserted. I went roaming about, moving quickly, and treading as if I would tread time under my feet, still half angry with you, and still longing, and longing, and longing for you. The hour went by, and still you did not come. You had told me when you were rested you would come out on the balcony. 'Come, come, come,' I said, 'and I will tell you everything. Every thought in my mind is longing to pour itself into yours.' Suddenly it occurred to me that the old man at the lodge had shown me a boat house, with some boats belonging to the Count in it. An idea came to me. We would dine at the lodge at six, and I would row you on the lake afterward. This gave me at once an excuse for sending up a note to you. I longed to be in communication with you, even through a sheet of note paper. I turned toward the hotel, for at the time I was looking away from it, and there, Irma, I saw you sitting in the balcony. You waved your hand. I went; I believe I ran toward you. I was upstairs, I was by your side in a moment; and your smile showed me how foolish my bitter dreams had been, and that whatever had tired you, you were not tired of me. I told you of my plan for our dinner, and our boating. You assented with pleasure; and then you said, softly and musically, as if you hardly knew you were saying it, as if it were a thought that had become embodied accidentally, 'Do you care for me? I thought just now that perhaps you were only amusing yourself.' 'I will tell you,' I said, 'on the lake what will make you think otherwise.'

"We dined at the lodge—you and I and the children; and afterward you and I went floating out over the water. 'Well,' you said presently, 'what are you going to tell me?' I said I was going to answer you the question you had asked me about Italy. I said, too, that you must be patient, and let me answer you in my own way. I began my story like this, as no doubt you remember: 'Since the days when you did your geography lessons out of a schoolbook, I daresay you have forgotten the very name of the city of Vicenza. It is little talked about; few tourists visit it; and yet, in all northern Italy, there are few places more interesting. Its narrow streets, blinded with Venetian shutters, are full of old palaces, having carved and pillared fronts, and great arches under whose shadow you enter, passing through them into stately courts. There are pale marble staircases, hushed and mysterious, leading to saloons and halls, whose ceilings are dim with paintings, whose great hearths are surmounted with carvings and coats-of-arms, and whose walls are darkened with old tortoise-shell cabinets. The roadways are overhung with rows of antique balconies, whose iron railings are twisted into leaves and lyres. There is a theater built more than three hundred years ago, which still has on its stage some of its original scenery. Lamps at night twinkle before the images of saints. The neighborhood is full of ancient villas, embowered in gardens. There are churches everywhere, full of twilight and gilding; and stray scents of incense meet you as you come round corners. You would think it the very place to dream in. Well—it was to Vicenza I went; and shall I tell you why I went there? It was to meet somebody to whom——,' Irma, when I said this you started, and exclaimed in a breathless whisper, 'Somebody whom you are going to marry?' I said, 'If you had asked me that question three weeks ago, I should have answered Yes! Wait a moment, and you will see how I answer it now.' Little Irma, what a true woman you are! Do you remember how you leaned forward, and exclaimed, 'Tell me her name. Who was she? I'm sure she was beautiful—and yet, no—I'm quite sure she was horrid!' I told you who she was; and you said that she was very grand, and that she was this and that, and that I had better go and marry her; and then you said, 'Well, go on. How did you fall in love with her?' I told you. I described her, and how I had felt about her, and how I did feel when I went to meet her at Vicenza. Then I described our meeting. I described her pleasure on seeing me—a pleasure so frank and placid, and the kind of pleasure I felt in response to it; and then I went on in this way: 'All that was good, and genuine, and intelligent in her, I recognized as clearly as ever, and the quiet high breeding that betrayed itself—or should I say hid itself? in every movement and gesture, and in every intonation of her voice. But, for some reason—I could not divine what—she seemed changed; she seemed faded; something seemed to have passed away from her; and I began to wonder what had been my condition of mind, when a girl like this could have tinged my dreams with rose color. Then we all of us began to explore the town. She and I were constantly apart from the others, and I tried to point out to her all the many things that touched my own imagination, and perfumed the very air with interest. One point I soon found out. So far as mere facts went, she knew a great deal more about Vicenza than I did; and small wonder indeed, for, as it turned out presently, she had just been learning by heart the contents of two guide books. But as to the sentiment of the place, as to that strange, plaintive music that old things make in ears able to hear it—of this she knew nothing. I had been at Vicenza once before by myself. I found it delightful then; but now, as I went through it with her, the same thing seemed to have happened to this town that had happened, so far as I was concerned, with regard to herself. Both, somehow, were disenchanted. Do you know, after two days' sightseeing, how she summed up her impressions? Vicenza, she said, is very quaint and interesting, but it would be a dull little place to live in. No doubt that last statement may be true; but it affected me when she said it exactly as I should have been affected if she had been to witness some wonderful religious ceremony, and had nothing to say about it except that there were draughts in the cathedral. Well—and now let me tell you this. All the time that I was there going about with her, conscious of disappointment, even before I acknowledged it, memories kept echoing in my mind of another relic of the past—an old castle in a forest on the borders of Hungary, where iron balconies overhung a forest of beech trees, and where I stood with someone who was looking for something that never came. That day I seemed to have moved in music; and I felt that now by contrast I first knew its full charm. That day was summer; these were frost. That day I was at home; during these days I was an exile. I was homesick, Irma, for our golden holiday. I didn't understand my feelings clearly then. I have learnt to do so since. I never said then to myself that the want in my life was you; but I began to find out, and to feel a secret relief in finding, that candid as my friend was, there was nothing in her manner which need necessarily mean anything more than cordiality. She felt that she did not, at all times, quite understand me. I could see this; and I could see also that she found in the feeling very little to discompose her. Indeed, I think that in a gentle, cheerful way she was amused by it. In saying this, I seem to be saying so little. In reality, I am saying so much. It came to this—that I grew certain of two things. One was, that though, if I made an effort, I might secure her affection easily; if I did not make that effort, she would be very little of a sufferer. The other was, that the effort was one which I could not make. Things being in this condition, fate did me a kind turn. My friend's mother had a sister who was passing the spring in Florence. This lady fell more or less dangerously ill; and a telegram was suddenly received from her by her relations in Vicenza, which, at a moment's notice, took the whole party off. Our parting was cordial—nothing more. I was left alone, divided between a sense of relief and a sense that my future, which had lately showed a definite prospect, had all of a sudden melted into stormy clouds.' Just as I was saying this, Irma, you gave an exclamation. Some large raindrops had fallen, and turning your face to the sky, you said, 'We are going, I think, to have stormy clouds now.' We looked about us. The sky had become purple; the stars were steadfast above us, and were wavering below us in the faint depths of the lake; but up from the west was floating a film of dusky vapor. Some more drops fell. We were not far from land, and we were both on shore before the real downpour had begun. We hastened into the lodge, where my room was already lamp-lit. We sat down. For a short time we were silent, and I was doubtful how to take up the broken thread of my history. By accident your eyes fell on a photograph lying upon my writing-table. It was a photograph of an old house. You took it up and admired it. I said to you, 'It is mine; but soon I shall have to sell it.' 'Sell it!' you exclaimed; 'your old family place! If I had a place like that, I would sooner sell my life.' There was horror in your voice, and also something like contempt. 'Do you know,' I said, 'why I shall have to sell it? It is my life; but I am going to sell it for the sake of another life.' Then I told you all. I explained to you, that so far as my fortune went, all depended upon my projected marriage; that this marriage I now found impossible, and that I found it impossible for a reason which I at last recognized—that reason being yourself. You looked at me as if you could hardly believe my words, and you drew a long breath, the sound of which I can hear now. You were sitting on a sofa, 'Bobby,' you said, and you could hardly speak for emotion, 'is this true? Come, sit by me here, and tell me so.' A little later on, you were saying this: and you spoke gasping. 'How can I be glad when you tell me I am ruining your fortunes? Is not this selfishness—the very madness of selfishness? And yet—and yet—oh, Bobby, you overwhelm me. No one has ever understood me, or ever loved me till now. I never thought that for my sake anyone could give up anything.'"

CHAPTER XIV.

IN the gray of the morning Grenville woke, with a dull sense weighing on him that a vague something had happened, which he shrank from looking at, and, when looked at, would change him in his own eyes. What was the life, the condition, the course of action, to which he now at last had definitely and passionately committed himself? And to what also had he committed her by the passion he had roused, and which he now knew to be so serious?

He moved to get up; but that would be to face realities; and he had not courage for the effort. He did so at last, however; his will rallied its strength. He hastily put some clothes on, muffling himself in his great coat. He softly unlocked the door, and he went out. The sky was a field of dim moving fleeces, damp as Gideon's, and so was the lake as well. All the ground was spongy and gray with dew. Nothing about him stirred but a slow and silent breeze, which just laid on his cheeks the touch of the weeping air. He looked blankly round him. In spite of its strange aspect everything spoke of her. He thought of their drive of yesterday, and the meeting of their sympathies in the sunshine; and then he started as his eyes rested on the hotel. Had it not been for that, yesterday might have been years ago; but that was a witness of her actual neighborhood, as it slept with its closed white curtains, and its wet tiles glimmering. His eyelids were heavy still; his head ached. How, he asked himself, would she meet him? Or would she meet him at all? Perhaps, he thought, his devotion would by this time seem to her to be an insult, and she would merely send him a letter, telling him coldly never to see her again. He looked at his watch. It was only five o'clock. Hours must pass before he could have any news of her.

Close to the lodge was a little patch of garden. There were some white roses in it, and some red tulips. He picked a bunch of these, and arranging them very carefully, went indoors, and put them in a tumbler of water. The cold air was now making him sleepy. He sought his bed again, and slept till Fritz awoke him. He made Fritz tie the flowers together, and told him to take them at once to Mrs. Schilizzi, and ask if she had caught cold owing to last night's rain. "If she wishes not to see me," he thought, "she will send back word to say so. I shall escape the humiliation of finding her door closed." He waited, miserably impatient, for the return of Fritz. He waited for half an hour. At last a message came to say that she was quite well, and would hope to see him soon after ten o'clock. Along with the message came a small scrap of paper, with this scrawled on it—"How good of you! what lovely flowers."

The words operated like a charm on him. A load fell from his heart. He realized that his coffee was at his bedside. He drank it, and rose instantly. He dressed with a hurried eagerness, and turned his steps to the hotel. As he approached it, his heart again sank, and his hand trembled as he knocked at the door of her sitting-room.

He entered; she was at breakfast with her children, and some of his flowers were in the breast of her red dress. She looked full at him; there was no reproval in her face; and her voice still had its laugh like the ripple of a brook in spring time. The only change in her— and, indeed, there was a change—was the growth in her eyes and smile of a clearer and more earnest affection.

"I see," he said, by way of saying something, "that Fritz has brought you my flowers."

"Yes," she said, pointing him to a chair at the table. "I know, too, why you sent them. Sit down and have some coffee with us. Olga, get him a cup."

Grenville declined. "Won't you?" she said. "You look tired."

"Do I?" he said; "I've been thinking."

"Yes," she replied; "so have I—thinking about many things. Come outside on the balcony. The children can finish by themselves. Tell me," she said, in a whisper, as soon as they were alone together, "do you mean what you said last night? You mean really that you will give your life to mine?"

Grenville looked at her in silence, as if vainly seeking for words: at last he said slowly, "I don't want to use exaggerated language."

She gave a gasp, as if a knife had wounded her. "Ah!" she exclaimed. "Then you were only laughing at me—tell me?"

"I don't want," he repeated, "to use exaggerated langauge; but I believe I am not exaggerating; I tell you that I would willingly die for you."

He was surprised himself, at the almost bald intensity which he heard in his own voice as he quietly said this.

The effect on her was like that of the sun reflecting itself in water. The returning smile on her lips, and the trusting affection in her eyes, which, deep as it was, seemed as if yet it were but half unfolded, filled him with something which would have been overwhelming happiness, if he had not, in consequence of his recent trouble and suffering, felt it as rather the blessing of overwhelming peace.

And yet, through all this, though he was scarcely conscious of the fact, some part of her was a disturbing and perplexing riddle to him—a riddle, however, which she herself could have answered, could she only have confessed herself to him as she did that day to her diary. For although she had calmed him, yet in a certain way she shocked him. He had feared she would have suffered too much. It seemed as if she had suffered nothing. But she, too, like him, had been face to face with self; and had confronted conscience with a braver face than he had, although she had expected an even keener wound from it. This, however, it is true, she had not experienced, and the cause was, not, indeed, the greater intensity, but the greater simplicity of her own emotion, and a certain moral fortitude greater than his, which it had endowed her with. What she wrote in her diary was as follows:

"In connection with a step I have taken, my own impression of myself is most vivid. One often reads imaginary stories of a soul's surprise after death at its own new condition, so wholly different from what was expected. I am like such a soul. Nothing has happened to me which, according to tradition, was sure to have happened. I have crossed a chasm into which I was sure to have fallen, bruising and crushing myself among the rocks; but something has borne me up—has carried me through the air. I am neither soiled nor injured. If I were I would confess it. I thought when I woke I must be; and expected every moment to find myself a spiritual wreck. As a fact, however, I found myself whole. Why should I pretend otherwise? I will pretend nothing. I ought to feel degraded; that may be—but I don't. I can say no more than that. And yet I can—I can say this. If I fail to feel what the occasion is supposed to demand, it is not from callousness. Were I really degraded, surely I should know the sign of it. I should feel unworthy of doing or of thinking anything good; my eyes would flinch from the thought of ideal goodness; and somehow and somewhere I should be hardened. But I am conscious of nothing of this kind. No—no. On the contrary, never has affection, or the sense of goodness and beauty filled my heart so full as they fill it now. My children to-day are more dear to me than ever. The desire for self-sacrifice, the desire for prayer, trouble me, and are ever in my heart. Even toward Paul my feelings have an unwonted gentleness; and it seems to me that to him I could give a more dutiful service, because I have found someone to whom I can give myself. I am not deceiving myself. I can distinguish good from evil; and my good thoughts and my pure thoughts—I knew them as my guardian angels. After the step I had taken, I feared they would have deserted me; but I look about me, and they keep me company still—as near me as ever, as much mine as ever."

Such then being her condition in her own eyes, what possessed her now was a sense not of abasement or trouble, but of exaltation. It was a sense not of a lost, but rather of a transfigured, universe; and Grenville's spirit adjusted itself under the direction of hers, as though it were stronger than his own.

"Bobby," she said to him, "I wish to be quiet this morning. We will come into the summer house, and you shall read to me."

He did so. There was beatitude in obeying her smallest wishes. He was not himself particularly in a mood for reading; but he found that this, for a reason which soon became more clear to him, did but add to the zeal of his obedience. Before luncheon, as they went back to the hotel, he picked up a broken flint, and with a laugh put it into her hands.

"Do you think that pretty?" he said. "Don't you? I wish you did."

"Why?" she asked.

"Because," he said, "if it would only give you pleasure, I would sit all day long and break stones for you."

After luncheon, she was tired and lay down; and he went away for an hour or so, in order to leave her quiet. He walked restlessly about the borders of the lake; and removed from her presence, the charm of which seemed to protect him, the first bitterness of his morning's mood revived in him; and when he went back to her, something had begun to stir in him, though he did not dare to recognize it, that was like anger against her. He did his utmost to disguise from her his changed condition; and his voice recovered its tenderness, but he could not recover his spirits. They had arranged to take the children for a walk among the shadows of the forest; and he tried to hide his dejection in his kindness and his attention to them. For a time this succeeded; but at last the truth was felt by her, his replies when he spoke to her were so short, and his smiles were so slow in coming. At last she said to him with a certain constrained abruptness:

"I know why you are so moody. You are afraid—though you might perhaps have thought of it a trifle sooner—that you have done me an injury by the hold you have acquired on my affections. Leave that matter to me. We have each enough to do to bear our own responsibilities."

To his morbidly sensitive ear her voice seemed hard and flippant. He hung his head and walked on in silence.

"Well," she said presently, "are you not going to speak to me?"

He looked at her, and was wounded afresh, by a smile that seemed almost mocking.

"Perhaps," he said, "if what you tell me is true, I had better go and bear my responsibility in solitude."

"If you like to," she answered, "certainly."

He stopped short in his walk, and fixed a long look on her. Then he held out his hand, and quietly said "Good-by."

"Good-by," she repeated, and turning away moved on. He remained where he was, leaning listlessly against a tree. A swarm of torturing thoughts at once sprang at him out of their ambush, accusing with hateful voices the woman from whom he was parting himself.

"You," they said to him, "are by no means her first lover. You are not the first in fact, and you have not even the first place in her fancy."

That these suggestions came to his mind like truths it is too much to say; but they irritated him like the sting of mosquitoes, with a pain which he despised while it maddened him. He looked after her to see if she were out of sight. She was not. She was at some distance, but just as his eyes turned to her, she too, stopping, had turned a glance toward him—a glance which, though still resentful, seemed to be full of melancholy. He hurried toward her, as though she were his life escaping him, which he must return to, though the process were full of pain.

"Irma," he said, "forgive me. My soul will kill itself if I leave you."

They walked on side by side, each of them still troubled. At last she spoke.

"It seemed," she said coldly but yet gently, "that whatever your soul will do, you could leave me very easily. I never," she went on presently, and her voice was a little harder, "I never knew a man take offense so quickly."

They had reached an open spot, where the children were picking bluebells.

"I am rather tired," she said. "I am going to sit down. May I ask you to spread my cloak on the ground?"

He did so, and sat down by her. Her recent speech had filled him with fresh bitterness, and inflamed anew the stings of all his recent suspicions. He was afraid to speak for fear of what he should hear himself saying; but at last, slowly and firmly, as if he were addressing a stranger:

"I am sorry," he said, "that my temper is so very

unreasonable, and that I show to so little advantage by the side of your former lovers."

She started in horror, and looked at him, as if she could hardly believe her ears.

"How can you," she gasped, "say a thing like that to me!" Her eyes held him motionless. They at once petitioned and judged him. They slowly filled with tears, and he saw that her lips trembled. Instead of reproaching him she helplessly leaned toward him, and resting her arm on his knee, explored his face wistfully. "Bobby," she said, "you shouldn't treat me like that. For your sake I have taken off my armor, and now you are stabbing me, after you have made me defenseless. Tell me—what is it? Why do you think bad things of me?"

He tried to explain. He did so very lamely; but she realized that he was reminding her of something she had said about "other men."

"I'm not perfect," she said, "I know that. I would willingly tell you all there is to tell; but it's not much. I've been interested in other men—yes, I have been interested; but that's all. Do you believe me? You must. It is the entire truth. I don't quite know," she continued, "what you are thinking about me. I have seen so much less than you. I believe I'm so much simpler."

"Irma," he said, "Irma, are you?"

"I think so. From you, at least, I have nothing I wish to hide; and you are the only person to whom I can say that, or ever could have said it. Once—yes, I must confess this—I thought I could have loved one man; but I didn't; and no man, not even that one, has ever so much as held my hand. Bobby—you must believe me."

Disbelief was impossible. He was conquered: he showed her that he was so. Her voice slowly changed to a happy murmur, which still suggested tears, but tears with a rainbow spanning them.

"I was like a dog," she said, "that had been beaten all its life. I trusted in you; and you were more cruel than anyone."

The words sounded like a reproach, but really they were the seal of a reconciliation. She seemed to be giving the keys of her heart into his hands—to be placing herself wholly at his mercy. Her soul lay before him as if it were clear water; he was filled by the sense of how wholly her whole being was his; and he felt that their union had been but half complete till now. The wood, which a moment ago had been chilled with gloom and bitterness, was once more full of sunshine and moss-scented air and flowers. This pair, lately so taciturn, sent out their voices to the children; and the laughter of the children, which answered them, was hardly more gay than theirs.

All through dinner that evening enchantment hung in the air. In the warm dusk afterward the children played among the glow worms; and then, when the nurse came out, calling them and telling them it was bedtime, Grenville and his companion again committed themselves to the boat, and noiselessly glided off together into the peace between the sky and water.

The boat was commodious, and Grenville, when he had rowed some way, shipped his oars and seated himself by his companion. They hardly for a time felt any need for talking. They each trusted the other to think and to brood in silence, each knowing that each was being taken into the other's life. All nature conspired to assist the process, touching them through their ears and eyes. Over their hearts was the cool of the immeasurable twilight. Stars were showing themselves— the immemorial friends of lovers; a young moon glittered like liquid silver. All around, the forests, softly dim and mysterious, guarded the lake, as they rose above their own reflections; and down in the depths below were the horns of the floating crescent.

In Grenville's mind what was taking place was this: An element in his devotion which had already made itself felt, but the nature of which he had hardly understood clearly, even when he had been most moved by it and had given it intermittent expression, was now coming to the surface, definite and recognizable, and growing in power as it did so. This was a longing which his passion had to express itself, not only in the enjoyment of her society, but in suffering for the sake of enjoying it. It was a feeling in some way resembling that of David, when he would not make an offering of that which had cost him nothing. Of its full meaning Grenville was not even now aware; but he knew this much, that one part of its meaning was a longing to prove to her and himself as well how intense this passion was, and to glorify it by the witness of self-sacrifice. "I would break stones for you, I would die for you." These had been fragments of the liturgy which was now inwardly completing itself. The mind became conscious of its own emotional changes mainly by means of a species of picture writing—a swift phantasmagoria of images, of metaphors and analogies. Grenville felt his passion to be mounting on wings, beating the dusk on its way heavenward, and taking her with him. And now, too, his condition flashed on him another unexpected facet. For the first time in his life he realized in his own experience how matter and spirit are capable of being fused together, how the body can rise with the soul instead of weighing it down, and how instead of dying it can be changed.

At last he said to her, "Let me breathe in your ear something. If every husband loved his wife as well as I love you, marriage would indeed be a sacrament, and earth long ago would have been heaven. If our love is degradation, there is no elevation possible."

"Bobby," she said, "why do you fret yourself? I know that my soul is living—now for the first time. You say you would die for me. My wish is to live for you."

She had arrived at the same self-knowledge as he had; only he had reached it gradually, by a conscious and difficult progress, through opposing prepossessions, which had to be met and reasoned with. To her, everything, though strange, had been entirely simple. She had not reasoned about sacrifice, or flesh, or spirit. Her thoughts were lost in him; she had ceased to busy them with herself. She only remembered herself, when his words had reminded her of it; and later on, when again they had reached the shore; and when, by and by, the doors of the hotel received her, she hardly knew that her feet had touched the earth, or that her cheeks were like fluttered rose petals.

Days and evenings now passed on without their counting them, varying little in respect of outward incidents, but witnessing, so far as the consciousness of Grenville and his companion were concerned, the formation of a new world either of reality or of illusion. Which it was, they had to learn by experience. Its formation was an experience in itself. From the first moment of his regarding her with any attention, he had not only felt her temperament to be attractive to his own, but he had discovered, under a misleading manner, that her intellect was active, and that her knowledge, though it was scattered, was curiously extensive. He now learnt how her education had been the work solely of herself. No guiding hand had been ever held out to help her. She had been the lonely sower of seed in her own soul; and some of the seeds had sprung up like wild flowers; others had hardly sprouted; and others, perhaps most, were sleeping. On these his thoughts seemed to descend like rain; and ground before that looked barren, began to grow green with life.

The precise nature of their relationship, and what might be its future consequences, never troubled them farther by presenting itself as a perplexity. They were insulated for the time from all external circumstances; and their life together appealed to their inner judgment only on its own merits as related to themselves only. In this isolated world, scrutinize it as they might, there was nothing to rouse in either of them any moral misgiving. Everything that either had imagined as spiritually or intellectually beautiful seemed to be sprouting and growing, and fulfilling itself. They seemed to be witnessing the days and dawn of a New Creation, and whatever they looked upon seemed to be "very good."

One night, however, in the boat, she said to him, after a long pause, during which her eyes had been fixed on the clouds and stars, "I wonder if—supposing people could see us—people, I mean, that the world describes as *good*——" She hesitated, and then went on, trying a different form of expression, "I mean," she said, "that, supposing we were not ourselves, I sometimes wonder how I myself should judge us."

"If you were not one of ourselves," he said, "you would, perhaps, judge us hardly, and the reason would be that you would necessarily judge us wrongly. The imaginary history which the world, if it looked, would make of us, would be a thing very different—how grotesquely different! from the reality. What are the thoughts that I, Irma, have offered you? Have I ever breathed to you one that was impure or shameful? Have I ever breathed to you one that was not half-brother to a prayer? My passion for you is worship, and my whole being is cleansed by it."

"Stop, stop," she said. "No, go on; go on. Do you remember what you told me once, that for people who loved truly you believed the heavens were opened as truly as they were for Stephen? Look up; look up. It seems as if they were opened now."

"Irma, Irma, can this indeed be living? It seems to me to be of so much more than life. See the depth above us, and the depth reflected under us holding endless space, and all the endless ages, and ourselves like a ball of thistle down floating between two eternities. Where that milky light is are new universes forming themselves—the book of their genesis yet remains to be written. From some of these stars the arrows that to-night reach us started on their vibrating way before Eve's foot was in Eden. Think of the worlds forming, think of the worlds shining, and the darkened suns and systems mute in the night of time. To us, to us, what can it all say, more than the sea says to a rainbow in one tossed bubble of foam? And yet, Irma, to me it seems that it says something."

"What does it say?" she murmured almost inaudibly.

"It asks, can it have no meaning, seeing that we are born of it? And can we be out of harmony with it, seeing that it speaks to us now?"

By and by that night, when he entered the lodge solitary, he heard himself utter aloud this passionate exclamation—"Can it be true? Can it be I am not dreaming? Is the rose indeed in my hands that I always had thought fabulous? Barren garden of life, bitter frostbitten furrows, can it be that you have bloomed for me into this one wonderful flower?"

CHAPTER XV.

Most people who have indulged in the amusement of watching the reflections of objects in clear water are familiar with the experience of seeing real rocks or pebbles force themselves into view through the visionary clouds or foliage. Grenville and Mrs. Schilizzi had soon an experience that was similar, when a packet of forwarded letters one morning arrived from Lichtenbourg.

They were at breakfast at the time, in her sitting-room with the children, and Fritz, who brought in a small budget for her, informed his master that for him there was another, which had been taken to the lodge. Mrs. Schilizzi glanced hastily at the envelope. Two or three she tore open, and read the contents indifferently; but she finally came to one at which her countenance changed. Grenville looked at her with a vague misgiving, silently asking her for an explanation. "It is from my mother-in-law," she said. "I don't know what to do. I really can hardly understand her. It seems she wants me at once to go back to London." She let the letter fall on her lap, and turned to him in distressed bewilderment.

"What has happened?" he asked. "Is it illness? Is it anything serious?"

"No," she said; "only business. I remember something about it; and something has to be done about which I have to be consulted—and—more important still—for which they require my signature." She showed Grenville the letter, and explained what she understood of the case to him. In spite of the rude break which it would make in their present existence, he saw that for her own sake it was really well that she should go; and he pointed out to her what she had not at first realized—that the whole business could be settled within a week. "Leave the children here," he said, "and ask the Princess to come to them; and before ten days are over you can easily be back again."

"And you?" she said, "what will you do?"

"I will come to England also. Who knows but that my letters may also contain a summons? I had but six weeks of freedom, and four have already gone."

For a little while she was silent, lost in perplexed thought.

"I feel," she said at last, "as if we had been sailing in a boat of dreams, and were now, with all that belongs to us, being lost upon the rocks of reality."

"Nonsense," said Grenville, with a vigor which approached roughness, but which brought to her, for that very reason, a certain sense of comfort. "If you and I are only realities to one another, we shall find that it is not our boat which is the dream, but the rocks, which you fear will wreck it. I will go to the lodge and look at my own letters; and when I come back, you shall see me in the character of a practical man."

There was every need, he found, for at once redeeming his promise. It is true that none of his letters was an absolute summons to return; but there were among them two important communications which made him see that his instant return would be desirable. One was from his man of business, the other from the Chancellor of the Exchequer. Both of them were serious enough in themselves; but quite apart from the actual news contained in them, they brought him face to face with a number of practical problems which he had known for the past week would ask now for a new solution, but which had till this moment seemed more or less vague and distant. All of a sudden they became close and tangible, and disclosed to him, as they did so, all sorts of troubling details. Returning to Mrs. Schilizzi he discussed their immediate movements. A messenger was dispatched to Lichtenbourg, who would go from thence to the Princess, taking a letter to her, and returning that night with an answer; and so soon as arrangements could be made for the proper care of the children, Mrs. Schilizzi would start, by way of Vienna, for England. At first it was assumed that Grenville would travel with her; but suddenly, with a doubtful smile, she said to him:

"Do you think you ought to? Perhaps I am foolishly nervous. I know the world so little, and I never before had occasion to be nervous at all. You must say what is best for me. I trust everything to you."

"Irma," he answered earnestly, "I need hardly tell you this; you already are sure enough of it. Were it not for external circumstances, I would never for a moment leave you. Every hour of my life I would be at your side caring for you. But in this case it may be best that we go separately—for part of the way at least. Let me think it over by myself, as I put my own things in order. My own things!" he repeated as he prepared to go back to the lodge. "How wretched to think that my things are for a moment separate from yours!"

As soon as he was alone he set himself to consider the situation. With regard to the journey he judged it best on the whole that he should precede her to Vienna, where he would meet her and her maid, and go from there in the Orient Express to Paris with them. In this way he would avoid meeting the Princess, who, since he had reached Vicenza, had heard nothing of his movements; and who, if she arrived promptly, as she might very possibly do, would be startled at finding him where he was in close attendance on her niece.

"How much happier"—the thought came like a cloud —"how much happier life would be, were there nothing in it that required concealing! Anyone, up till now, would have been welcome to find me anywhere. And yet," he continued, "we all of us have our burdens. Let me make the best of this one by the way in which I accept its pain."

Then with a sigh he let these reflections pass, to take up their lodging in some dim chamber of his mind; and others succeeded them, in certain respects more formidable, but yet of a kind which he faced with a better heart. These, but not the former, he recorded carefully in his diary.

"A man of an imaginative temperament," he wrote— "I have always thought this—may fill his mind with visions of the deepest and loftiest feelings, the tenderest sympathies, the purest principles, and acts of complete self-sacrifice; and connecting himself with these by an act of the imagination, just as he might connect himself with a character in a poem or novel, he will seem to himself to be a fine and sublime person, when he is in reality selfish and mean and heartless. Am I myself a person of that kind? If so, good God, to what a depth I must have sunk now! For nothing can justify me in my present condition but the fact that I am what I think I am—the fact that I mean my feelings. Do I mean them? Now comes the time for testing them; and I welcome the test. Suddenly, during the last fortnight, that strange catastrophe has befallen me, which when happening in the sphere of religion, is commonly called *conversion*. A something which I had always considered as something of secondary value has bewildered me by showing itself as the one treasure in life, and for the sake of securing this—so I have told my soul—I have already sacrificed much, and am prepared to sacrifice everything. But what I have sacrificed thus far has been merely certain scruples, which I have indeed respected throughout my life till now, and which I have certainly violated not without a pang; but so long as one's sacrifices are merely at the expense of one's scruples, they can hardly be accepted as much evidence of one's sincerity. I have felt this all the time. Again and again I have said to her, 'What I long to do is to suffer for you.' And my meaning I am sure has been—though I did not at first perhaps understand it fully—that I longed to convince myself of my own absolute sincerity—to convince myself that I was offering her my truth, and not my falsehood. Well, sooner than I thought, and more completely than I thought, the real trial has come. I see now that if I am genuinely devoted to her, if in any serious and self-denying way I mean to make my life the companion and support of hers, I shall have to sacrifice many things besides scruples. I told her that owing to her I should have to sell my property; and I knew when I said so that this was true. But I thought little—indeed I had hardly time to think of all that my words meant. I realize what they mean now. I have received a letter informing me that an offer for the whole property has just been made of a kind unexpectedly liberal. My lawyer tells me that if I am to sell at all, now is my lucky moment; and indeed I can well believe him. Such an offer would probably never be made again. I might have to sell on terms that would leave me a beggar. These will, at all events, make me sure of a competence. I must decide within three weeks. Within three weeks! so soon to part with everything! I feel like a prisoner who hears that to-morrow is the day of his execution. How near it is all coming! And a fortnight ago the entire prospect was different. Then, instead of selling my home, I saw before me the redemption of it. I saw life and honor returning to the old disconsolate rooms. And now it must all go; it must pass away like a shadow, pictures, furniture, everything, with some few exceptions. And why? For the sake of what? Is it not for the sake of a shadow? a shadow, a dream, a fancy of which the very memory will soon be unintelligible? If that were the case, I am certain at least of one thing; I should look on myself as a creature beneath even my own contempt. But it is no dream, no shadow, the thing for which I shall make this sacrifice. I know it was not. I knew that the feelings within me—the longing, the joy, the worship, the self-devotion—I knew that all these were no mere idle sentiment, but that for better or worse they were part of my very self. And now I am about to prove that my self-knowledge was true. Can my love be unreal, if I give up so much for it? Can it be selfish, if for her sake I am leaving all?

"I talk about *all*. I don't mean my property only. That is something; but I shall have to leave more than that. I think so, at all events; and at all events I am prepared to leave it. It is my new career that I am referring to. That would take me to Constantinople, and part me from her for an undetermined period. Irma, for those who are united as you and I are, there must be no separation such as this. Let me keep as near to you as I may, we shall be separated often enough. How often I cannot tell. The difficulties of our future till this morning were mere abstractions to me; and for the first time they are showing themselves as hard realities. They may be more, or they may be fewer than I anticipate; but be they what they may, I promise you this faithfully—there shall never be a day or an hour which I could possibly give to you, and which I will fail to give you, on account of what it may cost myself. The kind old man who would have acted so liberally to me about my marriage—the minister who has taken so friendly an interest in my advancement—to both of these I shall have to explain myself somehow; how I hardly know. I shall have, without the delay of a needless day, to let the authorities know that they must not reckon on my services. It will be difficult. There will be difficulties everywhere. And yet, what am I? I am so mad or so inspired—I have so completely lost my reason, or so completely found my soul—that all these difficulties, even while they fret and perplex me, and put an end to these weeks stolen from heaven, are at the same time filling me with exultation, and in every pang they inflict, are saying to me 'You are true to her.'"

He wrote this that morning, before rejoining her at luncheon; and he felt, having done so, more at peace with himself. Of the thoughts he had recorded he said little to her; but she felt in his manner a certain new quality which touched her, and soothed her, and gave her an added trust in him. He told her the conclusion he had come to, with regard to their journey; and though she winced at the idea of leaving him even for a day, she agreed that his plan was wise; and in the course of the afternoon she said to him, "If I liked you less, I should be more unhappy at parting from you; but the more I know you, the more of you enters into my soul, and will still remain with me, even when you are absent. Listen to me. I trust you. These are three short words; but all that is best and strongest in a woman's passion is implied in them."

Late that night the messenger who had been sent to the Princess returned with a letter from her, full of all sorts of kindness. She said, however, that to come to the hotel in the forest was an adventure beyond her strength; and she begged that, in their mother's absence, the two children might be sent back to the castle. "In fact," she added, "unless you telegraph to the contrary, I will meet you at Lichtenbourg to-morrow, in the middle of the day, and receive them straight from your hands, as you are on your way to Vienna."

"In that case," said Grenville, "I will be gone to-morrow, at cock-crow. I shall have the start of you by a few hours only. You will reach Vienna at midnight. I will call on you, at your aparments, next morning;

and that same afternoon we will start together for Paris."

They dined that evening at the lodge, without the children. "In thirty-six hours," she said, "I shall again be with you; but still, since we have been known and belonged to one another, this is our first good-by. Will you think me doubting and fretful if I ask you one thing? Are you sure you will be mine always?" There was a gentle solemnity both in her voice and look, which produced the sensation in him of being bound afresh to her—bound by a new link which was indeed unnecessary, but the added pressure of which he felt and received with gratitude. As he walked back with her to her door, she clung to his arm like a child, being taken to school, and about to be parted from its parent. The starlight showed on her cheeks something that gleamed like dew; and as she hid them and dried them in her sleeve, she murmured "I want never to leave you."

Grenville had to start by four o'clock in the morning. The sinking moon still shone as he dressed himself; but none of the lights of day were yet busy among the eastern clouds. The lamps of the carriage he was to travel in were staring with their nocturnal eyes; and he drove off behind the four jangling horses, feeling as if all the world were from henceforward to be night. Knowing that the sight would pain him, he turned to watch the hotel, as a man whose tooth is aching cannot resist touching it; and a desolating sense filled him, that though she would be soon restored to him, the conditions of their perfect union were done with, were lost forever. The mysterious forests, at first saturated with the darkness, and then as the wan dawn touched them yielding it up like an exhalation, would at any other time have charmed and aroused his fancy. But now every mile of the road meant to him one thing only—a return from Eden, into the forgotten troubles of life. Lichtenbourg, with its hotels and gardens, as he reached it in the ashy twilight, desolated him with vivid memories of his first days of acquaintance with it. Those days as he saw them now, were colored with the light of what succeeded them. They were vivid with hope and promise; but they were past, and their promise seemed vain. Horses were changed at the Hotel Imperiale, where he had stayed. The front doors were closed; but his mind through the shuttered glass saw the gleam of a certain brown hat and dress, which had appeared to him on the sunny morning of a day that fluttered with cherry blossoms. "Irma! Irma!" he constantly muttered to himself as he waited; and then presently the horses were put to; and whatever he muttered further, the bells and the wheels drowned it. When he reached the railway station he experienced another shock. His life of late had been so removed from the world and had given time such a new and expanded value, that though hardly a fortnight ago he had arrived at this very place, a train seemed as strange to him as if he had not seen one for years; and the musty smell which came from the red plush cushions of his compartment seemed to him the breath of our common unprofitable life. This journey to Vienna he compared dreamily with his last, when his mind was perplexed with thoughts about Lady Evelyn, stimulated with thoughts of his own brilliant prospects, and troubled—little as he at the time knew it—by her under whose influence all these prospects would evaporate. "I can hardly believe," he reflected, "all that has happened to me in a fortnight. All those interests I had meant to live for, and even the very world that holds them, I have already resolved to sacrifice, and am now on my way to do so. I can hardly imagine the value I once set on them. On the other hand, the thing which I value now, and for the sake of which I am renouncing everything else, is a pearl hid in a field which I flattered myself I should never enter."

When he reached Vienna about three in the afternoon, the change which had taken place in himself came home to him yet more vividly. The last time he had been there, and especially the time before, the very air of the streets had seemed to whisper of ambition to him. He had felt himself becoming one of the important figures of Europe, and about to be honored and welcomed as a part of its most stately life; while the pride of blood which underlay his desire of achievement had been stimulated there as it could have been nowhere else. But now all was different. The very reasons which formerly had made the Austrian capital, with all its glitter of to-day and all its traditions of yesterday, seem to him familiar and sympathetic, made it now seem bleak and alien. It seemed as if he had neither part nor lot in it. Under other circumstances, without losing an hour, he would have gone to the British Embassy to see the Ambassador and his wife; but now, though he thought of them still as two of his best friends, he shrank from the atmosphere which breathed through their bright drawing-rooms. It was once his natural element; he should now, he felt, be like a ghost in it. Far more answering to his mood was what he actually did with himself. He went to the offices of the International Sleeping Car Company and took three places for Paris in next day's Orient Express. In doing this he was conscious of doing something, not for himself only, but also for the woman he was devoted to; and the simple act seemed to be bringing him close to her. He even welcomed the fact that he had, out of his own pocket, to take an extra ticket, in order that she and her maid might be quite secure of having a cabin to themselves. That business concluded, he rambled through the town like a tourist, and presently bethought himself of going to the Ring or Boulevard, in which her apartment was situated, and taking a look at her windows. This he found, however, was hardly an attainable solace, as there was nothing to tell him which her windows were. They were somewhere or other in a huge block of building, whose frontage was rough with carving and gay with extended awnings, the entire upper part being devoted to flats or offices, the lower to glittering shops. Mme. Schilizzi's flat was apparently over the shop of a jeweler, and some of the objects in the window were at once so tasteful and splendid that Grenville for a minute or two stood in the street studying them. While thus engaged he was startled by the sound of his own name, pronounced with a charming though very foreign inflexion, and looking round he discovered the Countess C——, who seemed to have just emerged from the jeweler's swing-doors. She was full of questions, which she gave him no time to answer, and then of invitations, answers to which she demanded; but, finding that Grenville was only a bird of passage, and that he could neither come to her castle in the country nor join her in her box at the opera, she insisted on taking him off that moment for a drive in the Prater. Unwilling to yield, he had got no excuse for refusing. A huge engine of torture in the shape of a heavy barouche, with two gawky footmen in salmon-colored stockings, attending it, was there touching the curbstone; and this was presently bearing him away with the Countess, hardly more willing than Proserpine when she went from the fields of Ennes. Till they reached the Prater ennui was his chief suffering, but here ennui was lost in a kind of painful interest. As they drove through the crowd of carriages, or paused now and then under the trees, the Countess kept pointing out to him this and that personage, one great as a magnate, one fascinating as a beauty, whom he ought to know, and whom he would know, would he only stay in Vienna. Some of these desirable acquaintances stopped for a moment and spoke to her; and Grenville noticed in both men and women the same charm of manner which had at once attracted him in the Countess. Suddenly a carriage came by, the harness glancing with silver, and the servants breasting the air with gold lace and crimson waistcoats. It contained two ladies and a dark-bearded handsome man.

"Look," said the Countess, "there is the King of Moldavia."

Grenville turned, but it was not the king he looked at. What held his attention was two faces under parasols. Of one he only saw that it was middle-aged, refined, and cynical. The other he recognized by its wonderful velvety eyes—a face now set off by a dress almost insolent in its daintiness. Everyone as it passed gave it the homage of a stare. It was the face of Miss Juanita Markham.

"The woman with her," said the Countess, "is the well-known Baroness X———. I suppose you have heard *her* story. Your pretty compatriot is hardly to be congratulated on her friend; and as for the king, they say he is tiring of her already."

All this spectacle, varying, bewildering, brilliant, with a key to it here and there given by the Countess's comments, had for Grenville, no doubt, a degree of interest; but it pained and chilled him in two distinct ways. It made him feel how Irma was taking him away from it; and also how *it*, at the moment, was taking him away from Irma. His imagination, he felt, was being invaded by a vulgar crowd out of the street which divided him from her to whom all its domain was consecrated. "Irma! Irma!" he again repeated to himself passionately, but under his breath, and with a due mundane self-repression, so that the Countess who once actually caught a murmur, concluded that he was merely blowing away a speck of dust from his waistcoat.

At last his trial was over. The Countess dropped him at his hotel. The moment the porter saw him he put into his hand a letter. Grenville received it eagerly, fancying it might be from Mrs. Schilizzi. It was not. It was from the Ambassadress, who had somehow heard of his arrival. She begged him to come that night to dinner; there would be no party. He dispatched an acceptance, resigned rather than pleased; and, indeed, when the time came he was little less than miserable. His host and hostess talked to him much of his prospects; and he could not explain that they were now his prospects no longer. He was conscious of their wishes for his success, but their very wishes irritated him. He felt as jealous of any influence that would draw him from Mrs. Schilizzi as he could feel of any that would draw her from him. A strange sensation was dawning on him that his affection for her was, except for herself, making him alone in life. Wearied with the fatigues of the day, he returned to his hotel early, and was just preparing to close his eyes in sleep, and so to abridge the hours which still separated him from her, when the thought suddenly struck him that it might be a help and a pleasure to her if he went to the station and met her on her arrival. To rouse himself now was really a matter of effort; his eyelids were so heavy he could hardly keep them apart. But rouse himself he did, and redressed himself; and driving to the station, he awaited her. As the train came drifting in, he half feared that something would have detained her, and his heart gratuitously embittered itself with a pang of groundless disappointment. Among the dim figures that emerged he soon detected hers, and hastened to her glowing with sudden happiness. With a start of suspense and pleasure, she gave him her hand and looked at him, but the moment after the pleasure gave place to nervousness, and her voice, hardening and acquiring a note of petulance, "You shouldn't have come," she said. "Please go away and leave me."

"Can I do," he said, "nothing for you? May not I get you a carriage?"

"No, no," she said, almost turning her back on him. "Good-night; you can call at twelve to-morrow." And the next moment he saw her hasten toward a man—a tall corpulent man, whose hands glistened with rings, and who, with the aid of his nose, suggested finance and

Israel. With her hand on the sleeve of this gentleman's furred overcoat, she quickly disappeared in the direction of the cabs and omnibuses; and Grenville returned to the bed on which he had been about to rest himself, full of a bewildered bitterness which made rest impossible. He could not banish her strange reception of him from his memory. Her voice through the watches of the night kept ringing and echoing in his ears, and hour by hour its tone became harder and more bitter, till her image at last appeared to him, as he lay there half dreaming, like that of a woman who had suddenly grown to hate him, and having ruined his life was going now to spurn it away from her. The condition of his thoughts in the morning was somewhat calmer, but a sense of estrangement from her remained with him even then, and anxiety branded his forehead with its keen physical pain. But through all this he was famishing for her presence; and it wanted still a good ten minutes to twelve when he was standing at the door of the building in which her apartment was, and rousing the concierge with a peal of the electric bell.

"The first floor," said the man. "The first door on the right."

And Grenville, with trembling hand, was presently again ringing. A white-capped woman with an inquiring look admitted him, and, passing through a lobby in which the carpets were up, he found himself in a large drawing-room overlooking the street. There were no traces of life in it, except that on one of the tables was a pair of gloves and a parasol, both of which he recognized. He looked about him, full of curious interest. The floor was covered with thick red velvet carpet.

There were red velvet chairs and sofas, whose woodwork was sumptuously carved, but which suggested the fittings of an hotel, rather than of a private dwelling. The walls were papered with staring brown and gold, relieved only by two large mirrors and a life-size photoraph of the Emperor, liberally colored in oil. Here and there were some fine vases and candelabra, but they seemed arranged for sale rather than ornament; and the only other objects that decorated the shelves and tables were some ormolu trays for cigar ashes, some inlaid cabinets for cigars, and several sets of bottles and glasses for liqueurs, colored and gilt as gaudily as artists in glass could make them. One thing more he discovered, and one thing only. It was a photograph lying under one of the ormolu ash-trays, faded and ragged, and representing a half clothed Viennese actress.

Anything more depressing, anything more hopelessly *bourgeois* it would hardly have been possible to imagine. And this was the home, or at least, one of the homes, of the woman to whom he was devoting everything! He thought of the drawing-rooms at the Embassy, and compared them with it. They seemed to belong to two wholly different universes—designed for the lives of people who had not a thought in common. A surprise which he could not analyze at first occupied his mind, and made him forget how the time was passing; but at last it gave place to wonder as to when Mrs. Schilizzi would present herself; and wonder by and by gave place to impatience and resentment. Of all the troubles of life, the strained suspense of waiting, with every nerve stretched of doubt, of hope, and of hearing, in proportion to its real importance is the hardest for some temperaments to bear. Grenville's temperament was one of these; and it is no exaggeration to say that he soon was enduring tortures. Angry, savage thoughts came leaping into his consciousness, longing to assail the woman whose conduct seemed now so heartless; and he felt as he stood among them like a man in a cage of lions, trying to beat them down, to kill them, or to cow them into silence, and yet strong with a temptation to let them have their way. At last—and it seemed that he had been kept on the rack for hours—he heard, or he thought he heard, something like a distant rustle. All his senses of a sudden became hearing. He held his breath; he started; the door suddenly opened; and there before him, her eyes eager with welcome, was the woman for whom he waited.

She looked at him; she came up to him. She was wholly, entirely different from the distorted image which his mind had been just fashioning; but the stress of his late mood was still affecting his muscles, and his voice and look as he greeted her were, against his will, unnatural. She had greeted him as she used to do in the forest, at once gentle and passionate; and it was not for a minute or two that she took note of this change. At last she said, scanning him:

"What's the matter with you? Are you angry? Have I kept you waiting? Am I late?"

"No," he said, smiling in spite of himself, "only three-quarters of an hour. It wasn't that; only, after your anger last night, I felt rather doubtful if you ever would come at all. I thought, you see, that at the station I might have been some help to you. In fact I got out of bed in the middle of the night to come. You must forgive me for doing unintentionally what roused in you so much resentment."

For the first time the idea seemed to dawn on her that she had done or said anything which could possibly wound his feelings. A flush came into her cheeks, and a sudden moisture into her eyes, and putting her hands on his shoulders, she whispered, "Dear, forgive me. Come, Bobby, come, sit down by me. We are all alone —forgive me. But coming to meet me like that, late at night at the station, was calculated to put me in such a very false position, and it might easily have given Herr Silberman, a banker whom I happen to know, such a very cruel impression of me. You know you told me yourself how readily the world would judge wrongly of us. I felt so afraid and nervous, I hardly know what I said to you; and I trusted you so completely, I felt you would understand."

The trouble was over, peace had again returned to him. "In twenty minutes," she said, "I have told them to bring luncheon. Oh, Bobby, tell me, what do you think of this place? Isn't it dreadful? It will show you something of what my life is. Paul thinks it's beautiful. At first I tried to alter it; but it made him perfectly furious. He swore at me. He did more than swear. Look at my wrist. Do you see that faint scar on it? Wait a moment, and I will show you what is its history." She went to a drawer in a cabinet and brought out an ivory paper knife. "Paul," she said, "struck me with that, because I told him his room was vulgar, and wanted to put away those terrible sets of liqueur things. And there—I see, you've been looking at that photograph. The woman is Paul's great friend, and when I am away she reigns here. He thinks I know nothing about her, and this he must have left by accident. So far as appearances go, he is full of ideas of respectability; and he thinks that I ought to be ignorant that bad women exist. Ah!" she exclaimed sighing, and suddenly changing the subject, not as if in pain, but rather as if it repelled and wearied her, "how often when I looked round this room have I thought of our rooms at home—the shelves crowded with books, the chintzes and the faded carpets. Hark; here is Gretchen with the luncheon. When we have lunched you must go; and you must meet me punctually at the train."

This arrangement entailed a two hours' separation; Grenville bore it in peace. Their quarrel had made their union closer.

He was at the station before her, watching the passengers for the express, as they slowly assembled, and hoping they would all be strangers. He deputed Fritz to wait for Mrs. Schilizzi, to help her maid with the luggage, and to see them settled in their places. Until the train started, he had hardly done more than speak to her. No one could have imagined that they were traveling together by concert. She appreciated the quickness with which he had learnt his lesson. But as soon as the train was off and they both were perfectly satisfied that there was not a single passenger known by sight to either of them, they secured a sofa in the saloon which formed part of the Orient Express, and engaged a table for dinner in the restaurant car adjoining. It was five when they started in the mellow and golden afternoon, and the air from the gardens in the suburbs came with a gust of summer. In half an hour they were nearing meadows and wooded hills, vivid with exuberant green; and the shining curves of the Danube began to show and hide themselves, here reflecting a sail, here a town or a villa, and here the domes and façade of some palatial monastery. During their dinner they had drifted, not perceiving it, into the night; and the windows, instead of revealing the moving landscape, did but repeat the light of the lamps in the gilded roof. Mrs. Schilizzi retired with her maid to her own compartment, and Grenville shared his with a pasha and two Roumanians. The following evening, again in the warmth and sunlight, their eyes began to be greeted by lodges and blossoming gardens, and houses with mansard roofs. Then came buildings stretching in long white masses, and tall brick chimneys pricking the clear blue air. The train rattled over points; and they were soon stationary in Paris. To Grenville and his companion the journey had been a long idyl, and they had almost banished from their minds the doubtful sequel it was leading to. But an hour or two later, when after a hasty meal they found themselves seated in a crowded carriage for Calais, and heard the language of England spoken in several accents, when English newspapers were being called for and unfolded, and two puffy-looking men began making arrangements for going next night to a farce at a certain theater in the Strand—they felt for a second time that they had dropped down out of cloudland, and would have to face and struggle with the squalid difficulties of reality.

CHAPTER XVI.

MRS. SCHILIZZI was to be met at Charing Cross by her mother-in-law—a lady whose instincts always distrusted beauty, and who, strong in the virtue that comes of having never possessed it, felt herself bound, whenever circumstances admitted, to act toward her daughter-in-law the part of a guardian angel. Her zeal, indeed, was much in excess of that which a well-worn simile ascribes to the angels of tradition; and instead of contenting herself with keeping her charge under her wing, she endeavored to hold her in the grip of her guardian clutches. Grenville gathered this and more from what Mrs. Schilizzi told him. He accordingly parted from her at Dover, taking the train to Victoria, and engaging not to call on her till she wrote to him to give him instructions. Reaching London at six, sleeping for an hour or two, or trying to sleep, he found himself by twelve washed and brushed and dressed, and so far as externals went, ready to face the world; but the day that lay before him seemed blanker than the sands of the Sahara. He could hardly realize what time of the year it was, or in which of its social stages he might expect London to be. Had the season begun? Was it the Easter or the Whitsuntide holidays? What acquaintances should he find present or absent? These questions presented themselves, not because he wished for society, but for a reason precisely opposite. The social world, the world of dinners and parties, had become a thing which it was weariness even to think of. Could he have so arranged it, he would willingly have seen no one till the hour came when he should again see Mrs. Schilizzi. That, however, at the earliest, would not be till to-morrow; and meanwhile he had business matters to attend to, all of them fraught with pain, doubt, and embarrassment. He looked at the wall above his sideboard. His favorite painting was gone from it. He looked at a photograph of his home. His home was about to go. Some dusty cards of invitation were still sticking in his looking-glass. One of them bore the name of the wife of the Chancellor of the Exchequer. He remembered the party it referred to—his last before leaving England—small and brilliant; no common political gathering; and he thought of how he should soon return to the same house, not to fulfill but destroy the hopes that were then formed of him. His lawyer and the Chancellor—here were two people whom he ought to see at once, and for seeing whom he ought to prepare himself; and more formidable still, he would have to communicate with Lord Solway. But to none of these tasks, or the preparation for them, did he feel in any way equal. His mind shrank from them with an aversion at once weary and irritable, and wandered away to a certain suburban villa, till an impatient longing to reach it—a longing which he knew to be futile —threatened to incapacitate him for any other exertion. Presently, however, this weak and subdued condition aroused his own contempt; and by a strong effort of will he pulled together his faculties, and forced them to their distasteful duties.

First of all he began to write to the Chancellor, hardly

knowing, when he took the pen in his hand, what he was going to say, or what position he should assume. But thoughts, however scattered, are things which, in many cases, need only a severe enough summons to gather them together in an instant. Some men often wait idly for their thoughts to inspire their will; whereas what they really need is, that their will should compel their thoughts. Grenville found out this; and presently, to his own surprise, a letter was written which exactly suited the situation. With every phrase of regret that could flatter the person he was addressing, he stated that private matters, which did not admit of explanation, would prevent his going, at the time arranged, to Constantinople, and indeed had rendered his whole plans so uncertain, that he must renounce all claim to the privilege of serving the Government. There was another distinguished candidate for the post he had thus renounced; and he concluded his letter by saying that his worst regrets were tempered by the knowledge that his loss could be so well supplied. This letter he at once dispatched by messenger; and he then drove off to consult with his man of business. To renounce his career he found had been fairly easy. It was not so easy to write the irrevocable line, which would cut off from him forever the old home of his fathers, haunted with memories of his childhood and dreams of future children. He contented himself, therefore, with learning the terms of the offer made, ascertaining afresh the present condition of the property, and saying (though his mind was really made up already) that he should have to consider for a day or two before he came to a decision. "And yet," he said to himself, as he left his lawyer's door, "why do

I hesitate? A home—a home for my children! I forget myself. A man situated as I am, has no need of a home; or, rather, for him a home must be forever impossible. I must now write to Lord Solway and explain to him that I never shall have one."

This last was the hardest task of any; but again by force of will he compelled his thoughts to his service and he cut an easy way through difficulties he had fancied insuperable. He apologized for not having written earlier, to describe the upshot of his meeting with Lady Evelyn at Vicenza. He then explained that, far from having been able to propose to her, he had come to feel doubtful as to whether she even valued his company, and that before he could assure himself as to how matters really stood, her aunt's illness had for the time stopped everything. Here he suddenly paused, wondering how he should proceed. His letter thus far had the merit of being perfectly true; but as to his political career, how could he be equally candid? He could not palm off on Lord Solway a reference to "private matters," and tell him that a career in which he had taken such a fatherly interest was about to be abandoned for indefinite and mysterious reasons. "And yet," thought Grenville, "what is there I can say?" He detested falsehood; and it was impossible to even hint at the truth. At last he wrote as follows: "With regard to my appointment at Constantinople there is still much to be settled; and it is partly on account of that that I now have returned to London. My confidence alike in your kindness and your profound knowledge of the world, enables me to say to you what another might misinterpret as ungrateful; and this is, that all these affairs of mine, which you have so generously tried to forward, are now in a condition to prosper best by being left to slowly settle themselves, unquestioned and unnoticed. In saying this," Grenville added, after a moment's hesitation, "I need hardly ask you to forgive me."

This letter he sent by post, feeling no special desire to expedite its arrival; but when, having gone out for an hour or two, he came back to his room, he found an answer awaiting him, sent by hand, in the shape of an urgent invitation to dinner for the same night. He dispatched an acceptance. Hateful as the thought of society was to him, the leaden intolerable time that lay like a scorching desert between him and the earliest post by which he could hear from Mrs. Schilizzi, was worse even than society, and society would assist in abridging it. While he was dressing a large envelope was presented to him, from which he extracted a card for yet another entertainment—a concert in Downing Street, at the house of the Chancellor of the Exchequer.

The moment he entered Lord Solway's drawing-room, he saw that the party was one of the distinguished kind. There was no Royalty present; but the first person he recognized was a celebrated dowager, whose diamonds were generally a sign that a king or prince was in the neighborhood. There was more than one blue ribbon; and but one unmarried woman—the daughter of a widowed diplomat. Lord Solway shuffled up to Grenville, greeting him with a benignant smile, which however benignant to friends seemed to hint that it could be saturnine to enemies.

"You wrote me," he said with a sort of hollow

chuckle, "a very nice sensible letter. It contained one thing only for which you ought to apologize."

"What was that?" asked Grenville.

"Your apology," said Lord Solway. "Come—I must take you to the young lady—I don't know if you know her—whom you are to make happy this evening. Lady ——," he said, pausing before a magnificently dressed widow of sixty, "this is a young man dying to make your acquaintance. He's come all the way from Vienna to take you in to dinner."

"How silly he is," said the lady, who blushed and bridled till one of her chins overlapped her emerald necklace. "I've known Mr. Grenville for years; and I saw him at Vienna a month since."

She was indeed one of the luncheon party which Grenville had encountered at the Embassy; and, however absent or dejected he might be at heart, she left him at dinner no time to betray himself. Gossip and scandal, balls, liaisons and marriages, came from her lips sparkling like a succession of pearls; and she never had showed to greater advantage her talent for two things, which are not perhaps as different as might be thought from the names she gave them—picking people to pieces, and putting two and two together. Want of charity, however, has this advantage over charity, that it sometimes fails at last; and it did so on this occasion. Lady —— found toward the middle of dinner that the characters of all her acquaintances had died a painless death at her hands; so she left them in Grenville's memory, where she knew they would come to life again, and turning to her other neighbor, a widowed duke of seventy, renewed, with a well preserved archness for which she happened to be celebrated, an attack on his ducal heart, which practice enabled him to resist. In spite of himself Grenville was becoming amused. On the other side of him was the one unmarried young lady, with the eyes of five and twenty, and the happy *aplomb* of forty. Grenville knew her by sight, but he had never made her acquaintance; and he was pleasantly flattered, when she, the moment his widow had discarded him, met his eyes with a smile, and quickly began a conversation. She seemed quite aware that he had just come from Vienna, and treated his appointment at Constantinople as a matter of public news. She was acquainted with both cities, and talked about both pleasantly, giving her social judgments neatly, like the strokes of an artist's pencil, never laughing at anyone, not even the widow near them, but letting it be seen constantly that she could laugh if she chose; and all through this, by some subtle delusive means, not designedly, but as if by a natural instinct, she contrived to make Grenville conscious of two flattering facts—that she felt he was an interesting man, and that she knew he was a distinguished one. The anxiety and the longing for the absent, which was really occupying his mind, began to be overlaid and hidden by a little superficial pleasure, and after a time he felt himself taking note that the speaker's lips were pretty, and that her right cheek had a dimple. But the moment this crossed his mind, with a sudden and painful vividness, another image—other lips and cheeks—hovered before him like an image painted on the air. The first thing that reminded him of the charm of woman's beauty repelled him from the women present, glorifying the woman absent; and, completely for a second or two losing command of his thoughts, he actually found himself murmuring the words, "Irma! Irma!" He turned to his neighbor. She was looking at him. There was no help for it—he lied. "I'm right again now," he said. "I just had a twinge of neuralgia."

After dinner he fell an easier prey to a flattery, merely social, which he received from the elderly great ladies; and one of them who discovered that he had been asked to the concert in Downing Street offered to take him in her carriage with her. He went. There were many hours that still required killing. Before going to bed he wished to be absolutely tired, or he would not, he knew, get a single hour's repose. The concert tired him more than the dinner party. Several women, charming, young, and beautiful, showed themselves delighted to see him, and counted on his returning the feeling. The feeling was not at his command, but the manner and look proper to it, from mere force of habit, came to his aid and produced themselves; and anyone watching him would have thought on two or three occasions that he had fallen a happy victim to the eyes that were then detaining him. Several observers indeed did think so; but no observer could have known that at the very moment when appearances seemed most to warrant such conclusions the name of an absent woman was still secretly on his lips; and that the touch of a hand not hers on his arm, as he went to supper, sent through his nerves a shudder as if it had been some pollution.

The following morning, when his letters were brought to his bedside, it was some moments before he dared to look at them, he was so perversely fearful of finding that there was none from her. However, there was one. It asked him to come and see her at twelve. "I have told my mother-in-law," it continued, "that you know Lichtenbourg and the neighborhood; she is not surprised therefore at my wanting to make some inquiries of you."

In one way this delighted him. He would be with her sooner than he expected. He had, however, the preceding night promised his host to call at twelve in Downing Street; and there was some awkwardness in postponing so important an engagement. Postpone it he did, however, dispatching a messenger with a letter, full of excuses which were not perhaps very accurate. But the messenger had hardly been gone for half an hour when a telegram reached him from her, begging him to come at four. Here was a double annoyance—first the dreary interval thus suddenly thrust between him and the time for meeting her; and then a confused sense of that strange feminine selfishness which will allow a woman sometimes to disregard in a man's life every claim or interest not immediately connected with herself. For a moment there blew through his mind a little east wind of reproaches against her; but this went by, and without losing a moment, he hurried off to Downing Street, reaching it before his messenger. He was naturally before his time; and passed, as he knew he should have to do, a good half hour of waiting, which his thoughts made anxious and miserable. He tried to arrange precisely what he should say at the forthcoming interview; but every moment his considerations were interrupted by thoughts of her without whom he could hardly breathe. He tried to sit still, and amuse himself with a few blue books; but a physical weight seemed to be lying on his chest and smothering him; and his nerves constrained him to keep moving about restlessly. He could think of only one thing which would have given him immediate comfort; and that would have been to tear to pieces two huge blue books about the indigo trade, which he had twice taken up, and which nauseated him with their intolerable pages. But he stoically resisted this temptation of the devil; and a secretary at last appeared, and invited him to the sanctum of the minister. The result of the interview was more satisfactory than he had hoped. It settled nothing, and therefore was quickly over; and he went away with the news that, owing to certain recent events, it would be quite possible, if he wished it, to give him another two months before entering on his post or resigning it.

The clock was striking four when he found himself on the heights of Hampstead; and after much inquiry of the way, and numbers of misdirections, his cab stopped at the gate of a semi-detached brick villa, separated from the road by a walk and a few flower beds. As he rang the bell, a presentiment he was unable to conquer filled his mind, that she would not be true to her appointment; and he had prepared his mind for the bitterness of learning that this was so. The door was opened by a man servant, who looked like a dissenting minister; and when Grenville learnt from him that she actually was at home, the evangel that came from such a mouth seemed almost incredible. He was shown into a drawing-room on the ground floor, where French polish breathed from mahogany furniture, and antimacassars had settled themselves like a flock of sea gulls. There were some large but not beautiful pieces of Oriental china; some huge looking-glasses, hideous in florid frames; there was "The Lady of the Lake" in a varnished tartan binding; some calf-bound volumes of a ponderous quarto Bible; and on the chimney-piece, as Grenville at last discovered, some beautiful Greek vases, with figures of the Amazons on them, of Zeus and of Pallas Athene; but these, as it seemed from British ideas of decorum, had been draped in veils of opaque spotted muslin. This discovery saved him from the pangs of some moments of impatience; and he was still beguiled by a sense of unexpected amusement when the opening door startled him, and Mrs. Schilizzi entered. He had been secretly annoyed here, even more than he had been at Vienna, by being forced to connect her with surroundings so alien to himself; but the moment she now appeared, the effect of circumstances was reversed. Her dress, her look, her movement, seemed by contrast with the room to possess an added charm and refinement, giving her the aspect of an apparition; and her nearness to what was vulgar and tasteless showed him how completely she was detached from it.

Her eyes were soft with a glad ethereal welcome; on her lips was an eager smile; but as he approached her, she gave him her hand in greeting, with a curious coldness which effectually kept him at a distance; and with a quick, peremptory frown, "Don't come near me," she said. "You must sit there quite away from me."

In act he was completely obedient, but his mind was up in arms and rebellious; and though he still smiled as he spoke, and responded sufficiently to what she said to him, he felt his manner assuming a certain chill formality, which meant, "If you are distant, I can be distant too." As for her, had his judgment been only calm enough, he would have recognized in the tones of her voice and in the way her eyes followed him, everything that she had left unexpressed in her greeting. He would have recognized it also in something else, which did as a fact merely annoy him farther; and this was the sort of subject to which she managed to confine the conversation. She began talking about the vases. That was pleasant enough, and he really enjoyed a short laugh on the matter. Then she went on, "I don't know what you will think of Mrs. Grudden."

"Who is Mrs. Grudden?" he asked.

"Oh," she replied, "my mother-in-law! She married again after Paul's father died. She, you know, was English—as English as anyone could be. She was born at Clapham, and belonged to some religious sect there; and this room represents her idea of the beauty of respectable holiness. Everything is an expensive protest against beauty of any other kind. She and Paul's father quarreled like cat and dog; but, as soon as he died, she began to speak of him as a saint, and she kept those vases there as 'a souvenir of my dear first husband,' though I fancy she enjoys their petticoats partly as a slap at his memory. He brought them from Athens, and they really are very fine. Mr. Grudden, who died of a sore throat which he caught at a meeting for the suppression of dancing on the stage, was at first anxious to have them broken to pieces; but my mother-in-law, who resents all suggestions on principle, has often told me how indignant she was at this one; and then when Mr. Grudden timidly ventured on another, which was that they should be sent as a present to the British Museum,

'Mr. Grudden,' she said, 'I know my own business best. Were they sent to the Museum, their indecorum would be exposed to the public. Here, modestly covered, they at all events can do no mischief; and I can avoid affronting my dear first husband's memory, without feeling that I have any sin on my conscience."

In the way all this was said there was no trace of unkindness. There seemed to be in her nature a sort of gentleness which left her blows their precision but checked their force just as they were in the act of striking. Under other circumstances all this would have given him pleasure; but now, in his present situation, half separated from her, seeing her only in this breathless interval, he was longing to breathe to her some words of devotion and to receive from her the comfort of some answer; and her wasting this brief opportunity in gossip about Greek vases and a mother-in-law, began to fill him presently with a bitter sense that he was being trifled with. He tried once or twice to force her to speak more seriously, but each time she reverted to topics that were more or less trivial; and at last, stung with her treatment, and hardly reflecting on what he did, he arose abruptly, and said to her, "I have bored you enough. I must be going."

"Must you?" she said, startled, and looking as if she understood nothing of his mood. "What time is it? It is late. Perhaps you had better go, then."

He had not expected to be taken at his word like this. He stared at her incredulously for a second or two, and then, in a voice which she hardly recognized as his own, "When shall I see you again?" he said. "I will never come again, if you don't wish me to. I will never trouble you more."

"Bobby!" she exclaimed, "what can you be talking of? How silly you are! You had, indeed, better go now, unless you wish to see Mrs. Grudden." For the first time, as she looked at him, it struck her that there was pain in his expression. She came close to him, and taking him by both hands, with distress in her own eyes, she said to him, "What is it, dear?"

"I feel," he said, "that you have hardly let me speak to you, and now you turn me away, as if I were some chance visitor, and you will not even trouble yourself to tell me when, if ever, I am to see you again."

"Don't," she said, "don't remain any longer so near me. I feel as if all these mahogany chairs had eyes. You can see me to-morrow, I think. I have to go to my lawyer's, and you might take me afterward to some place where we can have luncheon. I will let you know to-night. Please don't be angry with me, but go."

Half soothed by her parting words and manner, and yet still embittered by the unnatural constraint of the interview, he went out into the maze of suburban roads, and heavy with a sense of desolation began to walk toward London. But a week ago—only a week ago—they were in that enchanted world of forest and lake and solitude, and now, he reflected, how great and how desolating was the difference.

The following day the promised letter arrived, and, having repaired at the hour named in it to the street where her lawyer lived, he waited for half an hour, and she at last came out to him. There was a well-known hotel in the neighborhood, and they lunched together in the coffee room. Confidential conversation was, under the circumstances, impossible; but there was something in her manner which spoke to him of her affection as plainly as words could have done, and perhaps more plainly than was prudent. But after luncheon she was obliged to meet her mother-in-law, and they parted without the solace of one single natural moment.

In the next few days they met in the same way. Sometimes she was tender with him, as she had been on this occasion; and not she, but circumstances, were the only objects of his resentment. But once or twice she seemed ill-tempered and absent; her business seemed so to preoccupy her as almost to put him out of her thoughts; and once, when he slightly reproved her for not noticing some personal question, she turned on him, saying, "What is it you ask me? Do you think I came here for the purpose of talking to *you?*"

That evening he wrote this in his diary: "We have two consciences—a moral one and an intellectual one; and most men, who have not silenced both, are not only accustomed at times to examine their condition, but from time to time see it in different lights. Both morally and intellectually, in a way I could never have anticipated, I have seen my conduct and my choice in life justified. That is to say, I have seen this at times. But putting the moral question quite aside, my intellectual conscience at moments exhibits me to myself as a fool. Here am I, deliberately—not in an impulsive moment— but deliberately, and with a careful and painful choice of means, preparing to divest myself of everything which the ordinary judgment would pronounce to be best worth living for. I am casting into the fire all that ambition craves for. The home of my family I am going to sell; and all chances of a better in another sense I am voluntarily thrusting away from me. And for what? This very morning, before I met her, I was with my own man of business, again going over the details of the proposed sale of my property; and when I met her, for whose sake I am doing this—good God! how does she receive me? I should have felt less pain had she stuck a dagger into me. No—no. It is not the pain I wince at, but the thought that her nature makes it possible for her to inflict it. And yet, all the same, I can plead for and make out a case for her; and then—here is the distracting part of the case—the moment I have done this I refute all my own pleadings, and represent her to myself as everything that ——. No, I won't think of it. But apart from this, how wretched my position seems. Three-quarters of an hour out of the twenty-four is all I now see of her; and these few minutes are snatched with difficulty, and preceded by hours of anxiety, as if all time was on the rack. And yet—and yet—if you are not the most contemptible of women—Irma, Irma, I should like to be saying this to you—if, in short, you are worth anything, to me you are worth everything."

Two days later he met her in a happier way, and so soon as the conditions were changed she changed also. She became like her former self. She wrote to him: "Call for me here at two, and we will go to my own house. I have several things to attend to; and I should like you to see the place."

This invitation to Grenville was like summer returned in winter. It is true that when she met him in Mrs.

Grudden's drawing-room she still treated him with a certain superficial coldness, but it was a coldness which her eyes belied.

"We will walk," she said. "It is the other side of the Heath. Come; I am quite ready. Let us be out of this dreadful room. As I told you the other day, my mother-in-law and all Paul's family seem to be staring at me out of these mahogany chairs." They were soon outside, and escaping from the region of streets, had taken a path over the broken and furze-grown heath; and now, as they seemed to be more securely alone together, her own natural manner, which Grenville had almost forgotten, came back to her.

"Irma," he said, "do you know how I feel now? I feel as if you had been dead, and had suddenly come to life again."

"Indeed," she replied, "I have been living under conditions that well might kill me." Her look and manner both showed that she understood him; but they left him sore with a sense that her sympathy was inadequate to his pain. "There," she said presently, "there is our house beyond those pine trees."

It was a large stuccoed villa in a garden full of foliage, with a gleaming conservatory on one side, and stables and out-buildings on the other. The drive and the flower beds were kept with exquisite neatness; some Guernsey cows were grazing in a quiet paddock; the stone steps that led to the glazed doors of the entrance were as white as a clean tablecloth. Everything presented the aggressive and painful neatness of a man who can think himself fashionable only when his clothes are new. Indoors Grenville received the same impression.

The floors were scrupulously polished; the walls smelt of paint and gilding; but at the same time he was astonished by the quality of the objects that surrounded him. There was in the hall a magnificent Italian coffer, and a huge picture, which purported to be a Rubens, and which, if not an original, was at all events a splendid copy. There were fine Florentine chairs, and a large Venetian mirror; and doors on one side opened into the conservatory, which was green with tropical vegetation. The reception rooms were just what the hall might have led one to expect. The ceilings were gaudy with Parisian clouds and cupids; there was abundance of modern furniture, which had been bought at an exhibition; some Sevres and Chelsea china; some marketable modern pictures; and placed about under glass cases some cameos, some crystal goblets, and other objects similar. Though nothing individually was first-rate, nothing was bad; but the effect of the whole was frightful. It represented a life altogether at variance with whatever beauty the individual things possessed. Grenville tried to keep this impression to himself, and merely said to Mrs. Schilizzi, "What a fine collection you have here!"

"Paul," she replied, "says there is not a thing that would not fetch now at Christie's fifteen per cent. more than the price he paid for it. Come—I will show you *his* room."

This was full of floridly-carved walnut furniture, much resembling that in the apartment at Vienna. It was all, as cabinet makers say, *en suite*, and the walls were adorned with pictures of race horses and ballet girls, and some shelves designed for books, but used for boxes of cigars. On the thick hearthrug was an electro-plated spittoon. All bore the same relation to the houses to which Grenville was accustomed as a schoolboy's nonsense verses might bear to a passage from Vergil—composed of the same materials, but differing in having no meaning. At last, however, a door was opened, through which he passed into a wholly different atmosphere. Here was a room, chill indeed with the tidiness that comes of being not occupied, but full of all the signs of delicate and refined life. The chairs were covered with old-fashioned flowered chintz; there were books in profusion, bound, not expensively, but with all the careful taste of one who evidently loved them. Over the chimney-piece were a few Chelsea figures; and on each side of the mirror were some cases of old miniatures.

"I have told the housekeeper," she said, "to let us have tea here. We can be quiet here for a little; and, dear friend, for a little I can be myself again. How horrid and how strange you must have thought me, these last five days. Bobby," she went on, "this room means to me an entire lifetime. It echoes with painful memories—with my first acquaintance with pain. And yet, compared with the other rooms in this house, I look back on it as a haven of rest—as a place where my heart ceased aching."

He began to look at her books, at her pieces of china, and her miniatures. She went round the room with him, standing by him and explaining everything. He saw the volumes she had valued most when a child, with the blots and pictures she had made on margins and title-pages. She pointed out to him her mother's miniature and her father's; and all the affection and purity which had brooded over her childhood, seemed to spread its wings over both of them, and fold them in a common shelter. "Irma," he said, "where shall I see you to-morrow?"

"By the way," she answered, "I wanted to talk to you about that. To-morrow I am quite free. Mrs. Grudden is going into the country; but the day after I am doing the same thing myself. That day is Saturday and I must stay away till Tuesday." An exclamation of displeasure involuntarily escaped Grenville. "Don't be angry," she said. "Why should you be so hasty? You can come with me if you like. That was what I was wishing to tell you. I am going to a little seaside place in Suffolk, to be for a day or two with a child of one of my sisters." Grenville's expression underwent an immediate change. This news, indeed, was beyond all his hopes.

"Of course I will come," he said. "But about to-morrow—listen. I have seen *your* home to-day. Will you come with me and see mine to-morrow? I am going to visit it, perhaps for the last time. It is," he went on, "only thirty miles from London." And he mentioned the railway by which to reach it, and also a convenient train. At first the expedition struck her as impossible. The fear of her mother-in-law seemed to paralyze her powers of movement; but the longing to come with him, growing as she thought over the project, presently showed her the means of absenting herself without offense.

At the appointed hour they met at Waterloo Bridge, and an hour's rapid traveling brought them to a Hampshire station, situated in a region of fir woods and wild commons. The dusty road, along which they were soon driving, was bordered with trees which made a flickering shade. Yellow gorse glittered; red-roofed cottages sunned themselves; and the signs of old-world inns swung by the broad footpath. The whole landscape was full of that singular primitiveness that is to be found in so many places that are almost within sight of London; and Mrs. Schilizzi was at once surprised and delighted at it. At length they reached a wide undulating heath, tufted with gorse and heather, and surrounded by belts of woodland, where white glimpses of several important houses showed in the distance, sheltered in the haze of trees. In the middle of this heath, at the beginning of an abrupt ascent, Grenville stopped the driver, and proposed to his companion that they should walk. He took her by a footpath up the slope through the gorse bushes; and the moment she reached the summit she stopped short with an exclamation. For there, on a slope beyond, backed by blue fir woods, and fronted by grass and fern, a forest of twisted chimney stacks rose from a dim red pile, whose magnitude was at once apparent from the number of its mullioned windows. Curious turrets in the garden, steps and balustrades, were visible. An avenue of elms climbed the slope to the house; and hardly a furlong off were the lodge gates giving access to it. "And is that your home?" exclaimed Mrs. Schilizzi. "How beautiful!" The words were ordinary enough; but there was a sort of sob in her utterance of them, full of thoughts and feelings which she was unable to speak. "And am I depriving you of this?" Such was its general meaning. Grenville knew that it was so, but affected to be otherwise occupied; and when he spoke he forced his tone to be cheerful. "Do you see this?" he said, as he pulled a parcel from his pocket.

"Yes," she replied. "What is it?"

And as she looked and spoke, he saw that a tear fell from her cheek upon her glove. He showed her, with a laugh, a false beard and whiskers.

"I don't," he said, "want to be recognized—in case there should be anyone to recognize me. I want to go as a stranger, and I have an order to view, which will admit us. Look—are the things on properly? I wore them at some private theatricals; and my oldest friends said that they would never have recognized me. Tell me—do you think you would?"

She assured him his disguise was sufficient, and not altogether unbecoming; and they went together up the avenue. It was evident that the place received a certain amount of attention; but signs of neglect and dilapidation might be nevertheless traced everywhere. There was a sheet of water covered with green weed; there were fences ill-mended; and clumps of trees and shrubs killing each other for want of pruning. At last came the iron gates, just outside the house. Half their scroll work was eaten away by rust. They passed through these into a great graveled inclosure, and made their way toward the lofty windowed walls, which the downdrawn blinds covered with blots of whiteness.

"My tenants," said Grenville, "I know are away now. I shall pass for a stranger—for an intending purchaser. I couldn't have borne to be seen in my true character. Everything here has for me some memory—every door—every window—even that old kennel there."

An echoing peal of the bell had meanwhile summoned a servant; and in the course of a few minutes they were making their tour of the house. On the principal floor, reached by a wide oak staircase, was a magnificent suite of rooms, hung with tapestry, and leading into a long gallery, full of old chests, and spinning-wheels, and the boots and breast-plates of cavaliers. To Mrs. Schilizzi the whole place was a revelation; and her breathless appreciation of it beguiled Grenville of his melancholy.

"We never," he said in French to her, "used to live in these rooms. We could hardly afford even to have them dusted. Our quarters," he continued, when they descended to the floor below, "our quarters were here, looking out on the garden." And the servant, as he spoke, admitted them to a good-sized drawing-room, hung with portraits, and surrounded with old gilt tables. On one of these portraits Grenville fixed his eyes; and then said hastily to the servant, "Pray open the dining-room—and the library, too, and the boudoir. I know the house—I shall have to see all of them."

The man went; and as soon as they were left alone, "Irma," said Grenville, "that picture is my mother. That is my little sister. Do you see this marble table, with a pack of cards inlaid in it? My mother was sitting by it, her head resting on her hand, the only time I ever said an unkind word to her. I was only fifteen then. I remember to this day the line of pain that quivered at the corners of her closed mouth. Everything speaks to me here. Don't think me a fool. I hope that man's not coming. I shall be too blind to see him."

His head was turned from her. He looked as if he were staring at the wall; but a moment later he turned to her, first biting his lip, then forcing a laugh; and there was nothing left in his eyes betraying a want of fortitude. Afterward they went into the garden, and then through portions of the park. He pointed out to her the bark of a youngish beech tree, on which some letters were cut, distorted by the rind's growth. They were still legible; and they spelt, "Robert Grenville."

"Come," at last he said to her, "come—we have seen all. When my mother and my sister died, I was fonder of this place than of anything."

"And now," she said, "for the sake of a worthless woman, you are going to rob yourself of all that was most dear to you."

"No," he replied, "a woman has revealed to me something that is dearer."

At a convenient spot he freed himself of his slight disguise. They rejoined their carriage, and the train was hurrying them soon to London. Her manner to him now had a tenderness he had never known in it before. Her being before had seemed to cement itself to his. It seemed to him now to be compassionately brooding over it. Poetry and prose came into strange contact. The sight of the signs and advertisements along the line, which showed them they were nearing London, suddenly roused her after a long silence.

"You," she whispered to him, "who are sacrificing so much for me, if I had courage, I should say to you, Do not complete the sacrifice. As it is, I can only say, let me do my all to repay you for it. I never knew till to-day how much you really cared for me. It has been a day of happiness, and also a day of trouble."

"Trouble is to love," he replied, "what the night is to a star."

"Vauxhall!" shouted a voice outside. "Tickets ready—all tickets!"

They both laughed at the interruption, and their parting at the terminus had peace in it.

Next day they again shared a journey, moving away from London to the quiet of the Suffolk shores. The melancholy of yesterday, the anxieties and jarring incidents of the days preceding, gave to them now a feeling of exultation, as if they were escaping from some house of bondage; and as for the sacrifice which had so lately saddened both of them, he had forgotten he had to make, she, that she had to accept it.

The watering place they were bound for was little more than a fishing village, with some villas, an hotel, and a terrace of lodging-houses annexed to it; and though in its season cockneys swarmed like flies in it, now it was full of its own local silence. Two musty cabs, however, were waiting patiently at the station, whose drivers appeared even more surprised than pleased when two well-dressed strangers appeared and engaged both of them. Mrs. Schilizzi was to stay in lodgings that had been engaged by her sister. Grenville had, by telegraph, ordered rooms in the hotel. The two abodes were not very far apart. They both looked on a wind-swept down or common, fringing which was the beach and the shining sea. On this common they had arranged to meet in an hour; and Grenville saw at a glance that there would be no chance of their missing each other. They met. After the jars and noises of London, and the painful and precarious meetings which, straining the nerves of each and trying the temper, still left smarting traces of the pain that had been thus inflicted, the intense peacefulness which now surrounded them lay on their ears like velvet, and found its way into their souls

The only sounds heard were intermittent and isolated—the occasional rattle of some solitary cart or van, or of one little yellow omnibus with the packages of some commercial traveler, the voices of a child or two playing, or of one man calling to another by name, or the fall of the waves which, long and slow and shining, curved into foam and fell on the shingle not far away. She took his arm confidingly, with a frank temerity, and they went toward the beach, over the thin, pale-colored grass, crunching with their feet as they did so many a drifted shell. Scents of the sea moved and floated in the air, and their hearts were filled to overflowing with a deep tumultuous tranquillity. They sat on the shore; played with the pebbles and threw them; and watched the dove-colored clouds change their shapes on the horizon, and catch the gleams of sunset.

"To-morrow," she said to him, "we will manage to dine together. This evening at six I must have tea with my little niece. You can dine meanwhile, and take me out again afterward."

At a little distance was an old wooden pier, dilapidated, and looking like the ribs of some wrecked vessel. An hour or two later they walked to it, when it looked black in the moonlight, and they sat together almost silent on one of its crazy benches. The tide was full. There was a hush on the breathless waters; and the heart of each had the hush and fullness of the tide. At last, however, Grenville roused himself, and instead of fragmentary whispers, began to speak with a distinct and deliberate utterance, which might to a passing listener have sounded entirely commonplace, but to her was far more convincing than the customary murmurs of sentiment.

"Irma," he said, "I wish, not for the sake of vanity, that you would think over certain merits, which I may venture to think myself possessed of. I am a good man of business. Were there any occasion for my doing so, I could go this moment into many a city office, and amend the details of many a financial scheme. I have a keen sense of humor and a certain amount of cynicism. I think also I am a seasoned man of the world; and no one has known better than I how to value the world's advantages; and I am certainly not mad. But my love of you—I am not in the least exaggerating—has acted like an alchemist, suddenly transmuting life for me, and turning my estimate of things entirely topsy-turvy. What I would utter to you if I could in all the language of poetry, I repeat, I engross, in bald matter of fact prose, and in cold blood I affix my signature to it. Nero wished that the people had only one throat, that he might cut it. All the things I care for have only one pair of eyes; and they are close to me—close to me; I see them shining now. Irma," he continued, his voice growing gradually lower, "my heart is like a cathedral, where a lamp is always burning in your honor, and where sometimes in honor of you there is nothing but solemn silence, and sometimes the murmur of some new act of devotion. Do my words reach you, so as to make you feel their force? Or are they like a jet of water, which breaks into faint spray before it strikes the object it is aimed at? If this is so, you must come nearer and meet it."

"Don't," she exclaimed. "Don't. Your words not only strike, but penetrate; and my heart is so full of what they mean, and so jealous of losing it—that—what shall I say? Bobby, I can hardly bear it. I am rather sad to-night. I will tell you why to-morrow."

To-morrow came; but the promise was not at once fulfilled. In the morning she was sad no longer. She was buoyed up on the tide of a triumphant happiness against which she could not struggle; and the horizon of the day before her was like that of a summer sea, which met heaven, and hid all the world beyond. Some hours she devoted to her little niece, doing for her all that could be done by the kindest mother; but every minute not thus occupied, she was with Grenville, full of a simple-hearted happiness which trouble dared not sully. But toward the evening her sadness returned again. They were sitting on the beach, watching some distant sails. Suddenly she said to him, "To-day you've been very good to me. You've not been angry with me because I've given so many hours to my niece; and yet I am sure it tried you. But you knew it was my duty; and you never once looked cross at me. I am so touched, dear, by all these little forbearances. And yet —O Bobby, Bobby, there is something I want to say to you. I wanted to say it last night, only I hardly knew how; and all to-day I've not wanted to say it at all."

"What is it?" he asked. She hesitated and blushed. She began to speak, and then stopped herself. What was in her mind Grenville could not conjecture; but one thing came better to his view than ever it had done before—the fact that for him she was guilelessly and defenselessly truthful. There was something almost painful in the degree to which this touched him—indeed the new and sudden call which it made on his care and tenderness. "What is it?" he asked again. "Tell me. I shall understand, whatever it is."

"Yes," she said; "I indeed believe you will. You understand me too well; and it—you are too good to me. I think I can tell you now. You see, Bobby, my loving you—you see sometimes it's mere happiness, just as it's been to-day; and then at other times it overwhelms me and lifts me like a religion. It was like that last night, and it is so again now. And this is what I feel—if we weren't in a public place, I should like as I told you to hide my eyes on your shoulder. I feel that the higher and purer my love gets, it raises some standard in me by which I condemn myself; or at any rate, it makes doubts trouble me, which in more careless moods I can answer. Don't be angry with me. I blame myself, not you."

"I myself," he said, "am not free from trouble. When I put before myself our position in general terms, often and often I condemn it; but when I think of it as it really is, and when I think of you as a part of it, let me say what I may to myself, it is redeemed, and my blame falls powerless on it. But oh, Irma, I ought to say this to you: If you don't agree with me naturally, I don't want,—how difficult it is to say some things,—I don't want to cajole you with what your conscience may resent as sophisms."

"Dear," she said, "I did not mean to distress you. I believe at heart I feel exactly as you do; but my doubts will come at times, and I like to tell you everything. But this evening, Bobby, they have come, not, I think, on their own account, but merely because my spirits are getting a little low again. I have a sort of a presentiment that something bad will happen to-morrow;

and even if it doesn't, to-morrow is our last day here. The day after I shall have finished my business; and then I shall have to leave you and hurry back to my children. To leave you—that will be sad enough; but not even for your sake would I stay away from my children. Perhaps if they were here I should have none of these morbid fancies."

"Irma!" said Grenville, "what have you just been saying? Do you suppose that when you go I shall not go also? As long as your welfare will not suffer by it and as long as you will allow me, I mean never to leave you. And as to your children—I should hardly believe that I had any place in your heart, if that place in some ways were not subordinate to theirs."

When they parted that evening, "Please," she said, "don't fret about me. Your goodness, though it sometimes troubles me, always drives away each cloud of trouble it raises." That night she wrote: "What a strange thing is the conscience! It often seems to me like the ghost of Hamlet's father, its voice coming now from one place, now from another quite opposite, as if it were urging on me two different sets of arguments. What a lot of books—scientific books—I have read about it, long before I thought that, for my own peace of mind, I should ever have to consider how far they were true. I believe, however, that I am really learning one thing, which I had often heard before but never realized; and that is not what conscience is, but what a woman is. A woman can appreciate reasoning as well as a man can; but it is not by reasoning that she sees her own way in perplexity. I can reason, and say that I am breaking some ties which, if everybody broke, all society would be

In the later stages it assumes a intensity — that the doomed provincial explains [?] a relationship — that clearly anticipates D H Lawrence.

258   A HUMAN DOCUMENT.

ruined. But then, again, comes an answer, I learnt from *him*; that if everybody loved as we loved, all society would be elevated. I constantly tax myself with making Paul miserable. But then again comes the answer, that this misery is merely imaginary, that it is merely the creation of some conventional formula, for I am merely giving to another what is nothing but dross to him. So, too, I can apply to myself all these names, which are the first stones cast by self-constituted accusers. But against names like these I hardly care to defend myself; I know them to be so inapplicable that they hardly cause me uneasiness. All they do is to turn me away from argument, and drive me back to my own consciousness of myself, which, in spite of every argument, remains still the same, like a flame inside a lantern which no wind can agitate; and then I know that my heart is not impure, and that the hunger of my soul is not to be faithless but to be faithful; that in spite of all the little selfishnesses that sully one's daily life, I long to consecrate my whole being to *him*. Even as I write now, some voice of the spirit fills me. That would sound nonsense to many people; but to me it is full of meaning. Words—words! where are you? Come to me, help me. If a rose has blossomed I can see it. If an aloe has blossomed I can see it. I can see that under his influence I myself have blossomed. It's a fact. Why should I vex myself by insisting on it any farther? As for arguments, they must play at see-saw if they will. They will sometimes make me feel that there is nothing to be said for us; sometimes that there is nothing to be said against us. But whatever is proved, oh, you who have chosen me and whom I have chosen, I know that I love you; and when I trust to my consciousness and my instincts, I feel that loving you was the first right thing I ever did, and that all hope and all elevation is contained in it."

Nor next day was her state of mind changed. The thought that this peaceful interval would so soon come to an end did, indeed, sadden both of them; but it was a sadness brooding over peace, like clouds over a quiet sea. The midday post, however, brought her a letter from London, bearing many stamps on it, and darkened with redirections. "It is something from Paul!" she exclaimed. Her cheeks flushed as she read it. "His work at Smyrna is nearly done," she said presently, "and—what is this? There are some new waterworks at Bucharest, for which the firm has a contract. He will be going there in three weeks. He supposes that I and the children are in Vienna or with the Princess; and as soon as he is able to do so, he will come to us."

She dropped the letter on her lap and looked at Grenville silently. "Of course," she said at last, "it must have happened sooner or later; but sometimes, Bobby, sometimes one forgets things."

"If you," he replied, "are as serious as I am, we both of us have to face a difficult and painful situation. I have known this all along; still, when a thing comes close, of course at first one shudders at it; but even if our path grows stony, do not the less lean on me."

As he spoke her smile again came back to her, but she only acknowledged his words by her sudden look of happiness. He felt that this gave him a new insight into her character. He felt that many things in her behavior, many little cases of what seemed neglect and carelessness, were due not to any want of recognition on her part, but to foregone conclusions that he would take her recognition for granted. And so through all that day, though a certain sadness filled it, a happiness reigned which the sadness only deepened. They arranged to dine late, so as to catch the last glow of the evening; and again they sat on the shore together, playing with the pebbles and the seaweed, and watching the waves fall. Everything on which their eyes rested was steeped in a pathetic beauty, which did not come from the sunset, though that indeed was beautiful, but which comes at any hour to things seen for the last time. She had been repeating some random fragments of poetry. Once or twice she had quoted a line wrong, and he laughed at her. Some sorts of ridicule are more tender than a caress. For one verse especially he insisted on finding fault with her. It was an English verse of eight syllables, and ought to have run thus:

> See, on the shore the waters fall.

She, however, turned waters into "waves," and he tried to convince her how halting she made the meter. Presently a thought struck him.

> See, on the shore the waves fall!

he repeated. "Do you know in itself that meter is pretty? I can't tell why, but my thoughts at this moment are in tune with it. Irma, be quiet a moment, and I will set them to the music of your mistake." He borrowed a pencil of her, and the back of an envelope; and now murmuring to himself, and now writing, he was occupied while she watched him. "Listen to this," he said at last. She leaned her hand on his shoulder, and watched his hasty scribblings as he read:

> See, in the west the day fails;
>   Low on the sands the waves sound;
> Slow on the down the lean sails
>   Of the mill drift round.
>
> See, in the west is one star!
>   See, a day we have found fair
> Is leaving the things that still are
>   For the things that once were.
>
> Hold me fast by your true hand;
>   Turn away from the changed sea.
> Our day forsakes the forlorn land,
>   Never forsake *me!*

THE END.

Printed in Great Britain by
Amazon.co.uk, Ltd.,
Marston Gate.